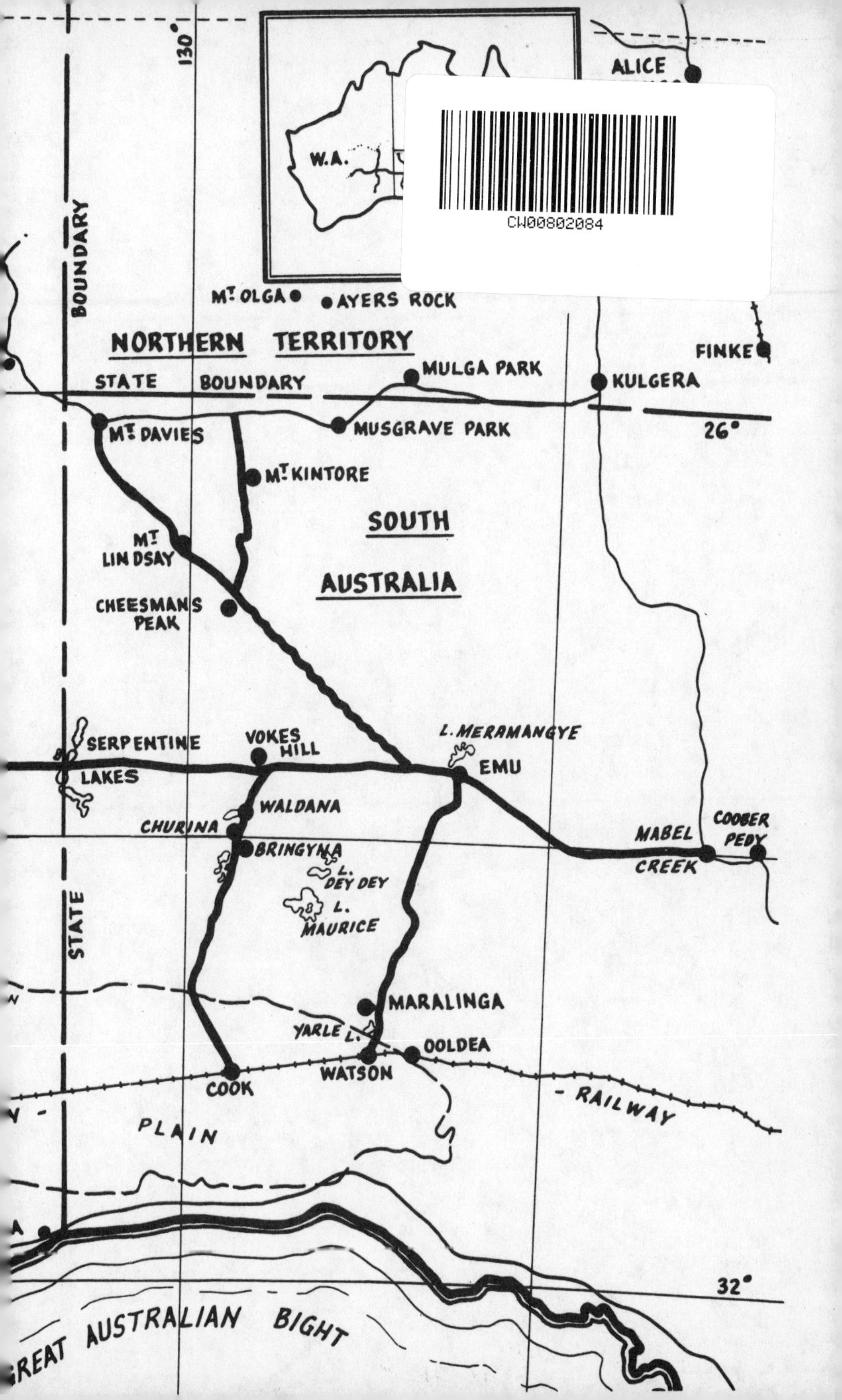
130°
BOUNDARY
W.A.
Mt OLGA
AYERS ROCK
ALICE
NORTHERN TERRITORY
FINKE
STATE BOUNDARY
MULGA PARK
KULGERA
Mt DAVIES
MUSGRAVE PARK
26°
Mt KINTORE
SOUTH
AUSTRALIA
Mt LINDSAY
CHEESMANS PEAK
L. MERAMANGYE
SERPENTINE
VOKES HILL
LAKES
EMU
WALDANA
CHURINA
BRINGYNA
MABEL CREEK
COOBER PEDY
L. DEY DEY
L. MAURICE
STATE
MARALINGA
YARLE L.
OOLDEA
WATSON
COOK
RAILWAY
PLAIN
32°
GREAT AUSTRALIAN BIGHT

BUSH BASHERS

LEN BEADELL

BUSH BASHERS

NEW HOLLAND

Books by Len Beadell:

Too Long in the Bush
Blast the Bush
Bush Bashers
Still in the Bush
Beating About the Bush
Outback Highways (a selection)
End of an Era

Published in Australia by
New Holland Publishers (Australia) Pty Ltd
Sydney • Auckland • London • Cape Town

1/66 Gibbes Street Chatswood NSW 2067 Australia
218 Lake Road Northcote Auckland New Zealand
86 Edgware Road London W2 2EA United Kingdom
80 McKenzie Street Cape Town 8001 South Africa

First published 1971
Reprinted 1973, 1975, 1976
Limp edition 1982, 1986, 1989
Reprinted by Lansdowne Publishing Pty Ltd 1994, 1997, 1998
Reprinted by New Holland Publishers (Australia) Pty Ltd in 2000, 2003, 2009

National Library of Australia Cataloguing-in-Publication Data:

Beadell, Len, 1923– .
Bush bashers.

1. Roads—South Australia—Design and construction.
2. Roads—Western Australia—Design and construction.
I. Title.

ISBN 9781864367348

625.709941

Wholly designed and typeset in Australia
Printed in Australia by McPherson's Printing Group

10 9 8

*To John T.C. Richmond, a lifelong friend,
without whose example and encouragement
from my boyhood I would not have started
out on this work*

LEN BEADELL, who has been called the last of the true Australian explorers, was born on a farm at West Pennant Hills, NSW, in 1923. After showing an interest in surveying at the age of twelve under the guidance of his surveyor scoutmaster, he began his career on a military mapping project in northern NSW in the early stages of World War II. A year later he enlisted in the Army Survey Corps, serving in New Guinea until 1945.

While still in the Army after the war he accompanied the first combined scientific expedition of the CSIRO into the Alligator River country of Arnhem Land in the Northern Territory, fixing the location of discoveries by astronomical observations. Later, after waiving his Army discharge for a further term, he agreed to carry out the initial surveys needed to establish the Woomera rocket range. It was this decision that was to lead to a lifetime of camping, surveying, exploring and roadmaking in the vast empty areas of Central Australia, opening up for the first time more than 2.5 million square kilometres of the Great Sandy, Gibson and Great Victoria Deserts. He chose the sites for the first atomic bomb trials at Emu and for the later atomic tests at Maralinga.

As Range Reconnaissance Officer at the Weapons Research Establishment he was awarded the British Empire Medal in 1958 for his work in building the famous Gunbarrel Highway, still the only East–West road link which stretches 1600 kilometres across Central Australia.

In 1987 he became a Fellow of the Institute of Engineering and Mining Surveyors (Aust.) and in the same year astronomers at the Mount Palomar Observatory in California honoured him by naming a newly discovered asteroid planet after him in recognition of the road network he created which made access to the meteorite impact craters they were studying possible. In 1988 he was awarded the medal of the Order of Australia in the Queen's Birthday Honours list.

The author of six best-selling books about his experiences in outback Australia, Len Beadell is married and he and his wife have three children, Connie-Sue, Gary and Jackie — all of whom have features of outback Australia named after them.

Contents

Illustrations

VOKES HILL

As I SCANNED THE UNBROKEN HORIZON of red sandhills and mulga from the top of Vokes Hill after finally rediscovering it, my first impression was that here at last was a place free from tax collectors and hydrogen bombs.

Binoculars were useless, as they only magnified the heat shimmer which converted the skyline into jelly as the sun blazed down on the already baked country extending for hundreds of miles in every direction. I was, at the time, in the middle of a hundred thousand square mile belt of dense mulga-covered sand ridges, completely bare of life apart from the few lizards moving from one salt bush to the shade of the next, with the nearest track of any sort some hundreds of miles to the south on the Nullarbor Plain. There was nothing at all to the west for almost five hundred miles, and three hundred miles to the east lay the opal fields of Coober Pedy, on the road from Adelaide to Alice Springs. Several hundred miles north was the road my little camp of six bush bashers had made, extending for nearly a thousand miles east to west. This was the first road bulldozed across Central Australia and was named the Gunbarrel Highway. I had originally called our band of men the Gunbarrel Road

Construction Party as a joke because, wherever possible, we liked to make our roads straight, and we felt quite honoured later to see the name Gunbarrel on the official maps.

It was at my present position in that stretch of desolation, where I did not exactly have the feeling of being hemmed in, that I had at last found the only labelled pinpoint on an otherwise bare map. By a series of astronomic and sun observations, I had been able to draw closer to the plotted position of Vokes Hill, observing stars with my theodolite at night, calculating the results by the lights of the Land Rover, and bushbashing it on the new bearing during the day. The sand ridges made it almost impossible to keep to any computed direction other than east or west, as that was the way the ridges lay, but by deflating the tyres to a point where any less would withdraw the tube valve, I was able to veer a little north and south.

Finally, I could sense the country rising, as from the top of some sandhills the visible horizon extending farther, with the sandhills and ridges becoming gradually more confused, lying one on top of the other, each starting before the other cut out.

The pattern was changing. That indicated that something had happened in the past geological ages to cause it all, in this case a build-up in altitude starting from many miles around and culminating in a crescendo of sand. A long time before, an expedition had been drawn towards this spot on its way—probably on camels—to a place where some mineral deposits had been mentioned by an explorer of the previous century. The word gold had been the incentive. This highest point in the turmoil of sandhills had been named Vokes Hill, after the man who had organized the trip. The expedition had struggled northwards from the bare Nullarbor Plain. At this moment I would gladly have exchanged my motor vehicle for a camel.

The night before, I had calculated my lat. and long., and after plotting them had found that the hill lay only a few miles by scale to the north-west from my lone camp. After mending the staked tyres and eating some bully beef from a

2

tin, I lay on my swag in the saltbush, impatient for morning to come so that I could get going once more. I planned to move west in a sand valley, following the ridge for a mile, then abandon the Rover in favour of hiking north for a mile or so to find this elusive summit.

By first light next morning I was again bushbashing through the heavy scrub in my unfortunate vehicle which I'd had modified with special reinforcements. Stopping a mile to the west, I took binoculars and compass and climbed up on to the first high sand ridge, from where I could see at least fifty miles south, but to the north all I could see was the next sand ridge a hundred yards away. Clambering up that, I could in turn see over the previous one, and after six more I began to see parts of a similar horizon away to the north. Plodding up on to each next obviously higher point, the time came when only one small section of the skyline out of the full circle was obscured. When I arrived at the base, where this final mound of sand met the confusion around it, I knew I had at last rediscovered Vokes Hill. It was impossible to walk up this last knob of forty-five degrees, so I crawled up on hands and knees with the sand not held by mulga roots cascading down around me. When I was next able to stand I was on the summit. The endless desolation, unobstructed in every direction, stretched away into the heat haze. I had no one with whom to share this final victory. In fact I hadn't seen anyone at all for a week, and then it was only the few men of my camp working at the head of our new road, servicing the bulldozer and trucks in readiness for the next onslaught which we had to make on the bush.

This was why I was here in the first place, to build a second road across Australia, also a thousand miles long, which would divide the continent halfway from the Nullarbor Plain to our original Gunbarrel Highway. The road was to provide access for a further series of surveys adding to the overall geodetic survey of the unexplored parts of Central Australia. The information was required for our rocket range projects at Woomera. Owing to the vastness of the wastelands in the semideserts of Australia,

3

such large-scale surveys had been next to impossible before the advent of bulldozers and four-wheel-drive vehicles. As these tellurometer traverses (so named after the new radar-style measuring instruments) require hills or high country from which to cover the distances, I had decided long before to make the road pass as closely as possible to the only point shown as a hill. This would help the parties from the National Mapping Council of Australia who would eventually follow in our wake to drive their heavy equipment near to any high areas.

So far the new road had progressed west from Emu, a site I had discovered for the first atomic bomb trials held on the mainland of Australia, to a distance of about sixty miles, and it was there that the bulldozer and camp now lay. Emu was joined to the Alice Springs Highway near the Coober Pedy opal fields by a bulldozed and graded road I'd surveyed and made several years before, so we now had two hundred of the present thousand-mile project finished, leaving only a mere eight hundred miles of road to make.

This we had planned to join over to Laverton in Western Australia which was almost a ghost gold mining town due west of Coober Pedy. Vokes Hill just happened to be right on line. That explains the trouble I'd taken to find it in that inhospitable wilderness. Astrofixes were positively the only way to do it.

Once the road was through and our survey needs satisfied, other incidental users of the road such as geologists, oil exploration parties, further state mapping groups, and Aboriginal patrol officers would be sure to follow. The overall help to Australia's future would be considerable, so I put as much care into the construction and survey location of these roads as if they had been much closer to civilization. I looked upon the whole undertaking as being much more of a privilege than a job, and would not willingly have changed places with anyone during the eight years I was engaged on it, although the work became very strenuous the farther we penetrated into the unknown.

Much support from our H.Q., the Weapons Research Establishment at Salisbury, near Adelaide, was needed and

4

given to carry out such an unusual and immense programme of work. One clerk turned pale as he ordered in for me a set of dental equipment with forceps and hypodermic needles used in teeth extractions. As I stood by his desk telling him what we'd need, he said he hoped he'd never have to join my camp himself.

The sun was on its way down at last and I thought it was time I should slide down the hill and start the trip on foot back to the Rover. I eased down the sand heap, starting a miniature avalanche which filled my open-topped hobnailed boots with the hot-baked grains. I emptied them for the hundredth time and retracked myself over the ridges back to the wagon. It was still there, glowing with the heat not only of the sun, but of the reflected rays off the ground as well as the switched off engine. It had taken several minutes to stop coughing after turning the key, so it all added up to an oven-like cabin. Again I had to shut the perspex windows against the mulga branches and sticks which constantly raked at the sides as I pushed through the scrub on the return to camp. The compass I had carried was only for reading magnetic bearings to distant rises or any features which served to draw up my own rough map as I went, and not really for use in finding my way through the bush.

A tyre had gone down while I had been away, and as I unloaded the ever-ready tools I realized just how thirsty I had become. I could now have a long drink from the tepid water in the tank, something I had made sure of not doing before the hike. It took a little manoeuvring to turn round in the scrub but eventually I was following my own tracks back in the direction of our camp of bush bashers. It was a great feeling to have located the hill at last and my thoughts now turned to that huge bulldozer blade which would soon be attacking the scrub, carving out the final road along which trucks could travel.

Apart from the complete lack of water, the hordes of flies, and the utter remoteness of this wilderness, it was relatively easy camping country. There were not many problems such as hairy poisonous spiders, snakes, or other dangers to combat. All you had to do for a fire was to rake your fingers

5

along the ground and light the resulting heap of hot dry tinder. In other areas it takes quite a project to get a fire going with soggy wet wood, each piece harbouring some specimen of insect ready to bite or strike their venom into unsuspecting fingers. Clouds of the more disconcerting mosquitoes also take the place of our flies which at least go to bed at the same time as we desert dwellers do. It is only one night or two a year that rain disturbs us, although at times I did think a little more would be welcome.

During the quarter of a century of almost continuous camping in the open, I often wondered what another might do while searching the stars every night before sleep took over. I happened to occupy myself with the forming of countless patterns of right-angled triangles with the brilliant pinpoints of light filling the black sky on moonless nights, and it was only on the full moon evenings that I would forcibly have a rest from my geometry.

After more silent, lone camps and a dozen flat tyres, I eventually emerged from the scrub to rejoin the camp at the head of the road to date, and found everything ready to be on the move again. Doug, the bulldozer driver, ambled over to see how I'd got on, while old Paul, the cook, put on a billy. Scotty made an exaggerated burst of running to his grader, as if not to be left behind, and Frank Quinn, the supplies driver, yelled out from underneath his truck that it was about time I got back from stargazin'. Rex, the heavy equipment fitter, knowing everything was in first class mechanical order, didn't need to stir from his conference with Eric about some worldly topic. Eric's job of cherry-picking, or cleaning the finished road free of hidden roots, stumps, and loose sticks was now about to resume, but he'd been just as hard-pressed helping Rex with the machinery.

They were an extra good group of men whom I had picked from places as scattered as the Maralinga bomb site, the Northern Territory, and farms a hundred miles east of Adelaide; they included a former bush shearer's cook who had been working in Mines Department water drilling camps. As Scotty had once said during one particularly rough period we went through soon after our little band got

6

together: you need bush blokes for the bush jobs! Some of them stayed with me for eight years, under the worst conditions possible, during our work in Central Australia, and then the couple who did leave did so reluctantly for family reasons. Most of us were single, without a tie in the world, but Doug had to go and get married and spoil it all, eventually followed by Eric, and then even myself. Rex just sat back contentedly, telling us how sorry we'd be, but I noticed he was as happy as any of us although he had been married for many years.

We were eventually to make four thousand miles of roads through the unexplored Centre, but here now was our latest project, that of joining east to west across Australia for the second time.

A survey link from the Gunbarrel Highway to Emu had been required before beginning this one, which entailed a road of three hundred miles starting at Mount Davies, a point near the north-western corner of the State. We had finished that. Being in a south-easterly direction it crossed over hundreds of sand ridges with which we were now battling.

Anxious as we all were to get on with our new project, yet another road had to be made from the Vokes Hill area south to the Nullarbor Plain, and we arranged to do that first. It was a direction which meant these sand ridges had to be crossed every hundred yards and the scene as viewed from the Hill didn't hold out any hope for an easy going. The first thing now was to close the remaining gap from the present camp to Vokes Hill and tap the resulting road at the best looking spot for the bushbashing south.

We made a start the same afternoon that I lumbered back to camp, and it was with great pleasure that I watched the huge cat 'dozer fighting with the scrub in place of my relatively delicate vehicle. The first section was travelling with the sandhills, and irrespective of the thickness of the scrub we usually managed to carve out about four miles each day, double the width of the blade to protect the truck canopies from overhanging mulga branches.

Ahead of the bulldozer, I had the chance of deciding on a

7

place I'd planned to call Vokes Hill Corner, and settled on a spot a few miles short of the place where I'd left the Rover to complete the recce on foot. It was still in the heavy scrub, but the sand ridge on the south had cut out, giving us a few hundred yards' start before attacking the next one, so after the bulldozer had crashed through the trees to that area, we guided it a hundred yards farther on the route to Vokes Hill.

That was to be as far as the road would go west, until the new one was opened up south to Cook, a siding on the Nullarbor Plain on the Trans-Australia Railway Line. Backtracking then to the exact spot planned for the corner, we cleared the area of scrub ready for a camp and started the bulldozing towards Cook. This was only to put our little base camp clear of the future roads. When the first sand ridge loomed up, the heavy machine again back-tracked and continued east to the head of the road where the trucks were waiting for something to drive on. Vokes Hill itself would still have to wait for its road as it had already done for so many thousands of years.

The next stage was to chop a heavy log of black oak for a sign-post, carry out an accurate astrofix for its lat. and long., and attach the aluminium sign plate I would make for it. When the camp moved up and settled in, it was time to start yet another expedition to see what we'd be in for on this job. While unwanted equipment was being sorted and unloaded, I prepared for the trip. In this country I wasn't altogether looking forward to it, with the dozens of staked tyres I was bound to run into.

We planned to have the party move back up to the Gunbarrel Highway to carry out a regrading programme of parts of it that were reported to have suffered in a recent downpour of rain while I was away from them for several weeks after this new expedition.

The reason was that it had become my turn to copy Doug, despite his advice about how to avoid weddings, and I had somehow been included in the arrangements to take place in several weeks' time. All I had done was to allow myself to be persuaded into purchasing a house in which I had no intention of living and had returned to the bush leaving behind a family kind enough to occupy it for me. The fact that they had a daughter led eventually to this present planning at Vokes Hill Corner.

After the expedition then, provided I got through alive, I would be going to Adelaide, and as I ploughed off into the scrub I was not sure just what the sad expressions on the boys' faces meant, but I made a shrewd guess it didn't have anything to do with the rough trip I had just begun.

The going was quite as hard as I had known it would be, and each high sandhill required a dozen attempts to finally cross over, while the thickly covered carpet of mulga trees raked along the sides of the Rover. One branch pushed right through one of the perspex side windows and from then on I was sitting up to my waist in a nest of dry sticks as they poured in through the jagged gap. The non-magnetic rods I'd designed running from the front reinforced grille to the top corners of the windscreen protected the glass as the bulk of the branches slid up and over the vehicle, but I still resembled a nesting wedge-tailed eagle.

On one crossing, while backing down in preparation for the next attempt, the Rover slewed out of its wheel tracks and I found myself side on to the rise, with the vehicle on the point of overbalancing, held up only by a small mulga tree growing in the sand. I was on the lower side, and the angle the door made with the ground made it impossible to open it enough to get clear. This meant gently crawling over the transmitter and other boxes on the passenger seat to climb out through the other door, and with a shovel and axe it took an hour to relieve the excitement of possibly watching the Rover rolling over and over down the hill.

There were some native wells indicated on the way, which I had no hope of finding on this trip without much observing of stars but which I endeavoured to come close to on my recce. I would find them later, if possible, and make the road pass by them as a means of location for future parties following along, labelling them with the usual aluminium plates. I carried quite a number of these together with a set of alphabet stamps for this purpose, and when the lack of trees for posts made it necessary to bolt them to lids of empty diesel drums, I'd shoot the holes through with my revolver.

The rippled mulga green carpet effect as seen from the higher ridges stayed with me for a hundred miles until I detected traces of marine limestone on knobs in the valleys which had been exposed as the wind had blown away the loose sand. This meant the vague first beginnings of the Nullarbor Plain, made up of marine limestone from the middle miocene period with an age of about forty million years.

The scrub was still thick, but the worst of the ridges were behind me now, as were the maze of dry salt lakes I'd been forced to weave through, and it was only a matter of time before I could expect to emerge out of this mixed up jumble, known as the Victoria Desert, on to the bare plains.

It had been a week since I'd left the boys and I could see a lot of hard work ahead to make this access a reality, but it was a challenge as well. The mulga was as thick as I'd seen it growing anywhere, and camping in it this last week made me eager to see proper daylight around me each morning, instead of the gloom of the mulga jungle, as I emerged from my swag roll. Gradually the scrub opened up as the outcrops of limestone took over, until suddenly it stopped, as if a giant mower had been used, and I could see a fifty mile clear horizon for the southern half of the circle. The last bushbashing and sandhill expedition I was to make as a free person was over.

After driving across the plain to Cook and continuing on in the direction of Adelaide, eight hundred miles away, I began to wonder nervously if it were not, after all, easier to cope with the country around Vokes Hill.

A FEW UNPLANNED DELAYS

RETURNING TO THE DESERT wasn't as easy as I'd imagined. But there was still plenty of work waiting, so I rejoined the party camping on the Gunbarrel Highway as Scotty carried on with the regrade. To our amazement we found that the Musgrave Park cattle station had been built right across our road, by the Aboriginal Affairs Department for the natives in the reserve. Their idea was to prevent just anyone driving into the natives' area without first being checked for the necessary permission by the resident superintendent. And my road, therefore, passed roughly through the lounge room and kitchen of his homestead. So with our grader handy on the spot we made a small loop road around for them, and also by arrangement with our H.Q. and the Department of Native Affairs, we offered to construct an airfield for them.

All this was further delaying the building of our second road across Australia. With equipment such as ours on hand, however, these were the obvious and practical things to do. We were further delayed by a quick trip to Giles for the purpose of extracting a tooth from one of the members of the meteorological party there. He was in dire straits with the pain, and it was only 300 miles away! After adding the twenty-eighth notch to my forceps I was at last able to locate a site and make a survey for the airstrip two miles from Musgrave Park.

We took the grader to the first survey peg to begin the construction. Then Scotty began to feel sick and couldn't climb on to his grader—a "crook stummick" he complained of—so the airstrip had to wait once more while we drove him back to see the Flying Doctor. He would be landing fifty miles away on the Mulga Park cattle station airstrip which we had graded. A radio message was sent to inform the Alice Springs base of Scotty's symptoms, and as a result of the meeting several bottles of gaily coloured pills were added to our stocks. The doctor attended to some natives with sores, checked up on the owner's "expecting" wife, and assured us that Scotty would almost surely live.

If the "stummick" had waited another week, a hundred-mile return trip could have been saved as he could have landed on our new strip at Musgrave Park. But then we would have missed an incident at Mulga Park . . . an incident that could only happen in the bush.

While we waited in their kitchen for the doctor to examine Scotty, the cattleman was standing by the warm stove fire reading a cowboy book. A china clock, attached to the wall by a screw, hung over the row of treacle tins containing tea, sugar—anything but treacle—on a shelf over the stove. In the quiet, still room and without warning or explanation a loud crash rang out. The china clock lay in a thousand pieces on the concrete floor. The station owner dropped his book and whirled, sure that Billy the Kid had finally got him. Everyone stared at the screw still firmly in the wall above a clean circle in the dust where the clock had been. It had hung there for years. Things like that just have a way of happening in the bush.

Back at Musgrave Park, Scotty was sufficiently over his trouble to resume operations on the grader to begin the airstrip, and soon we had carved out the mile-long centre line with over-runs heading off either end to clear the rocky hills of the Musgrave Ranges. For this project, of course, we had the services of dozens of natives who would benefit by regular visits of the plane; their job was to cherry-pick the runway clear of sticks. In three days we had a field forty yards wide—including a windsock pole—and ready for use.

The time had come when we could return to Vokes Hill to start on the road to the Nullarbor. It was almost five hundred miles away by roads we had made, but with all the heavy equipment the main Alice Springs to Coober Pedy road would be quicker, as it saved crossing the hundreds of sand ridges over which ours had to pass. From there we would be able to drive the three hundred miles west through Emu to where our bulldozer stood waiting at Vokes Hill Corner. It would still be easier, even though that way added several hundred miles to the journey. But we were not yet destined to leave, for another drama was starting to take shape.

It appeared that one of the staff there, the bookkeeper and governess, was having fears about being shot to death by her husband; he had been on the warpath ever since she was forced to leave him through lack of furniture. Her story didn't make too much sense for a while as she was a little upset, but it seemed that each time they had a difference of opinion, he'd break a chair over her. As these differences seemed to be frequent she'd finally grown tired of standing up all the time. She hadn't bothered to advise him of the date of her departure or even of her intended move and had gone out to the bush in search of stronger furniture.

The trouble was that she had confided in a relative about going, and when her husband had come home one evening looking forward to breaking something, he was so disappointed at finding her gone that he sought out the relative. Afraid that he would do the same to her own furniture, she had told him all about it. With that he'd gone off and purchased a rifle, packed his bag, and travelled to Musgrave Park. While we were finishing off the airstrip a letter had arrived for the governess, setting out events leading to the rifle transaction and it eventuated that any day now the "Musgrave Kid" should arrive, armed to the teeth with not only the rifle but also a permit to proceed to the homestead. Another letter followed, from her energetic partner, stating he was on his way.

The station superintendent mentioned that a little support from us could help to enable her to maintain her health, so of course we stood by. We all conferred on the best way to handle this situation, our ideas ranging from hiding her up in the mountains until the danger had passed to waiting for him with a tribe of natives brandishing spears. However, most of the ideas proved impractical, so we arranged for the meeting to take place. Then we would ensure that no gunplay came into the picture. What happened after that was up to the two of them.

In one of our Land Rovers, Eric was to scout ahead for signs of the truck bringing the man and the suitcase in which the rifle must surely be. Then he was to come back to let Scotty know on the waiting grader. Scotty would stop his machine on the road in the thickest clump of scrub blocking the way and sit working at the engine. Eric would then have time to tell us at the house so that everybody could take up their places to prevent that suitcase being opened until things were sorted out.

In the bitter cold of the following morning, Eric came hurtling along in his Rover to inform us the suitcase was on its way. Excitement mounted as everyone took his place. Scotty dived for the grader and was off. Rusty revolvers were produced and stuck in waistbands for effect. The governess sat in the kitchen wringing her hands and staring at the door to the first-aid room on the verandah.

Within half an hour the mail truck trundled in amid a cloud of dust, and a man wearing a tie jumped out clutching a suitcase. As he started for the house across the dusty flat, the suspense must have been too much for the governess. She came running out and across to meet him half way. We all kept our eyes glued to the leather bag which was dropped in the dust as a conference took place in the middle of the "arena."

He didn't look strong enough even to lift a chair, but soon they both turned towards the house with him holding the case in one hand and his wife's hand in the other. It was all over as quickly as it had happened and we endeavoured to act as if nothing had happened, which in fact was the case. He

14

informed us that all he'd bought was a pig farm in New South Wales and she had agreed to return to it with him. He looked a little bewildered at being asked if he had a good supply of strong chairs, but replied that the farm house was indeed furnished.

The last we saw of them was when they boarded the mail truck in the icy cold wind on the following morning and drove away in a cloud of dust. He was sitting on a petrol drum in the back huddled up in a saddle blanket against the cold with his suitcase alongside him, while she sat in the warm cabin with the driver. We never did learn what was in that bag, but as they were lost to view in the billowing dust we had no fears for her safety on the pig farm.

The map of the airstrip and homestead, together with their latitude and longitude which I'd prepared, was finished ready for issue to the air authorities. At last we could be on our way south to the bulldozer. We'd even mended the frame of Paul's glasses where they'd broken across his nose. I had done it with the same material I used for mending plates on false teeth; he didn't mind the pink join on the tortoiseshell circles one bit. As long as he could read books out of his "tea chest" library he was happy.

As we lumbered away from the station with our trucks, trailers, and grader we thought that whatever we were in for must be dull compared with life at Musgrave Park. We were proved wrong; nothing could ever be dull in the bush. Soon the waving group of our black and white friends were obscured in the ever present volumes of fine red dust.

At Mulga Park, where we stopped overnight, the events of the stay at the Musgraves were related, but I missed most of it being outside observing stars for an astrofix of the homestead there. Pilots and mapping parties had often requested this information so I couldn't miss the opportunity of obtaining it once and for all.

There was time next morning to make a wooden face for the china clock, which still hung on the screw minus the china, with its hands pointing out in mid air. You had to guess what hour it read and often the natives would have an extra long wait for their marmalade and damper.

It looked at last as though we could be on our way, so with Quinny driving the truck towing our little refrigerator trailer, and Paul in the ration truck, we continued on the trek. The grader kept in front of us all to set the slower pace, and as usual Rex came last with all the tools, spares, and fuel to keep us going. Soon after the mugs of tea at Victory Downs homestead ninety miles farther on, and a retelling of how the desperate Musgrave Kid was foiled, we were on the main road travelling south.

Now I reckoned that in another couple of days we'd be back at the bulldozer and on with our work, but it was still not to be. As I was coming along behind the truck and fridge trailer in my Rover just clear of the dust cloud, I noticed a wheel racing off across a cane grass flat. At the same time a tow bar reared up out of the dust ahead for an instant, to be immediately replaced by an axle and then a canopy. End over end went the trailer ahead, and as Quinny stopped the dust settled, revealing a heap of wreckage lying on its side near a cane grass swamp. The wheel which had broken off and had caused all the damage was still spinning away into the distance. I took off in the Rover after it to catch it before it stopped moving and became lost in the tall cane grass of the dry swamp. I found it with the broken stub axle still attached, and hoisted it on to the bonnet of my vehicle for the return journey across the swamp to where Quinny waited studying the mess. When we opened the door, the scene in the freezer box was one no housewife would care to find . . . the walls, roof, and floor were coated thickly in a mixture of eggs, fat, cheese—all the ingredients needed to make omelettes. That gave us an idea for our dinner so we shovelled some of the mess into a pan and fried it. It tasted all right to Frank and me, but the others, when they arrived, thought they'd try something else. Scotty had returned on the grader wondering at the lack of dust following along. His only remark was, "Here's something you don't often see."

Two logs from the tray of the truck served as a ramp up which we could pull the quarter-ton fridge trailer by means of a cable, one end of which was attached to the trailer, and

16

the other to the grader. This would mean another interruption to our work, as we would have to cart it all down to Maralinga from Emu on a road I'd made before, to have it mended. A three hundred-mile return trip to Emu added to the eight hundred miles to begin with . . . that bulldozer would be getting mighty lonely.

Five hundred miles and several days later we struggled into the workshops at Maralinga, where a crane lifted off the rubbish so the fitters there could try to restore it to normal. In order to work on it and breathe at the same time, they first had to steam-clean the box where the broken eggs had taken on rather a different odour.

Eric, Paul, Rex, and Scotty waited up at the atomic ghost camp of Emu where they serviced the rest of the vehicles. Quinny and I made the detour to Maralinga.

For several nights we slept indoors—a rare thing for us— and while the trailer was being remade another delay occurred. As I had carried out the initial surveys for the new series of atomic bomb tests there, and as I was on hand with my instruments, I was elected when a further test site was being prepared. While Quinny helped in the workshops, I was out each morning surveying from my own pegs, extending the original network to incorporate the new series of trials. This meant calculations each night; I wondered what I'd done that was so bad as to deserve this.

After I had completed this incidental survey, and the results and figures had been handed into the people concerned, I found the job of restoration to the trailer was finished; the unit was not only freezing once more but it was capable of being towed. This was where Frank would be making regular visits from our camp to draw rations, fuel, and water, so the stop-over got him familiar with his set of contacts.

Eventually the time came when we felt that nothing more could possibly keep us from our bulldozer and we were at last able to leave Maralinga, loaded down with rations and fresh water for the trip to Emu and Vokes Hill Corner.

Always after passing through the old atomic bomb site at Emu, I felt a sensation of acute depression because it held so many vivid memories of that year so full of action when that first atomic blast had ripped through the country. I remembered the hundreds of scientists bustling about all bent on the one job of exploding the bomb and recording the results. It had been such a lively place made happy by the enormous pressure of work which had a rigid deadline; busy men in the bush are always contented men. I had first discovered the site in virgin bush never before visited by white men, and from that day onwards the place had grown into a large atomic tent village with the eyes of the world upon it. Now it was as dead as yesterday's headlines. Blistering sun and harsh weather had reduced what little was left to termite-eaten ruins and the new site at Maralinga had claimed anything salvageable for re-use there.

I'd made the 150-mile road connecting the two sites myself, so truckloads of equipment could be hauled out leaving any unwanted pieces to rot away in the desert. It was on this road that Quinny and I had just travelled, so it was to help us also considerably on this new project, making me realize more than ever how like building a house our work was. We'd do something, then add to it, and further plans and projects could be made and added to our existing work again. The satisfaction of looking back on work we had achieved and making use of it kept the group of bush bashers going, despite complete absence of easy working conditions. We could all share in this, and the more we did the greater the urge was present to continue onwards against almost impossible odds.

As we drove into Emu I thought how deadly the radio-active dust around the actual bomb had been just after it had gone off, in a sequence which had been initiated at the touch of a button. We decided to make the trip out to see what it looked like now. The English scientists who had visited the area since with instruments had left finally, assuring us that the area was safe, so we had no fears concerning radiation. It was a fifteen-mile drive on roads I'd surveyed and made before the activity had started, and passing the row of Mustang aeroplanes we'd used in the test, we stopped on a rise a quarter of a mile short of the smooth saucer-shaped circle of melted sand. The devastation from the bomb was still as it had been on the morning of the explosion but with the addition of clumps of saltbush growing again in the "saucer." It looked harmless enough now, but in the centre of the clearing I saw in my mind's eye the hundred-foot-high steel tower we'd built; the bomb had rested on this a microsecond before it had vaporized the tower in the first flash. I could still hear that dramatic count-down bringing to a close two years of intensive work, my work and the amazing efforts of the British atomic team, led by a man who is now Lord Penney.

The row of Mustangs were showing the impact of the weather. I remembered how they had been flown in one after the other for observing the effects of atomic blasting. Placed far enough from the tower not to suffer the same fate, they had been rendered, as I thought, incapable of ever taking to the air again. But later when I had written my book on the project, I learnt how a group of ambitious men had read it, and had arranged with the authorities for the planes to be salvaged. Before that of course no one knew of their existence. It eventuated that these men had actually resurrected them and flown them away. They must have been first class aero-mechanics.

Driving slowly back to the derelict village site on our way out west, I knew there could never be another year like that one, and I was elated to have been so closely connected with it all.

The salt bore water had solidified the taps in the old shower recesses and rusted out everything it had touched, including the plumbing. The bore casing in the ground was silted over, with the pump rods and toothed wheels above locked solid. Once those bores provided the whole camp with its water supply for a year. It was altogether a sorry sight.

We had made an all-weather airstrip close by on a natural claypan. The presence of the latter had led me to decide upon the site in the first place. It was still suitable for the landing of sizeable aeroplanes. The windsock pole remained, but shreds of canvas hanging from an iron ring were the only evidence of the sock itself. The ironwork of the control tower on a sandhill overlooking the strip still stood divested of the wooden room, once on top, from which all the comings and goings of the aircraft were directed.

The skeleton of the stage we'd built still stood, drooping and leaning at all angles. We had put on many lively impromptu concerts there. The stage on which I myself had stood cartooning camp characters on white butcher's paper with lumber crayon in front of an audience composed of the whole tough crew, was crumbling. It was full of large gaps where the sun's rays had beaten down, as the white ants had devoured the savoury woodwork. The cipher room from which all the top secret messages had been sent, including one to Sir Winston Churchill after the successful explosion, was also a ghostly ruin. I just wanted to get away to the new projects waiting for us at Vokes Hill.

As we drove off to the west to cover the last hundred miles of our journey I was again reminded that it is always better to stay away from such places, preserving only the more pleasant memories.

After another night's camp our exhausted little party, with all our clumsy looking equipment, crawled on to the clearing we'd made at Vokes Hill corner. There was the great bulldozer right where we'd left it. There were weeds growing through the caterpillar tracks in the sand indicating to us just how long it had been since last switching it off.

Of all the delays due to airfield construction, dentistry and surveys, crash-ups, weddings and near murders, not to mention the medical examination, clock-making, and astronomy, only one had really been planned.

Our sign-plates will tell future travellers where they are

The bald rock mountain at my "oasis"

ROADS MADE WHILE YOU WAIT

It wasn't long before Rex had the bulldozer refuelled, filters changed, track rollers greased, and the pilot motor running. Doug pulled up the decompression lever when the oil pressure was up and the huge diesel started first time, proved by the jam tin placed over the upright exhaust pipe flying through the air. The tin was always used to keep out the weather, rain, and sand storms. Soon the great blade lifted at the touch of the winch lever. We were on our way and I went ahead of the hundred or so yards we'd already 'dozed to guide the machine over the first sandhill crossing, within easy view of Paul cooking tea.

At the end of the cleared start we'd made south, the blade lowered like the head of an enraged bull and crashed into the heavy mulga scrub towards my flashing mirror on top of the ridge. In this case it could be seen above the scrub, but on flat going the thickness of the growth prevented the sun's reflection from penetrating, making the use of a signal pistol flare necessary. Carrying on over the ridge and down into the valley between it and the next, the machine turned around with its blade this time at ground level and picking up a load of trees, branches, and sand, it cleared that section

At our own most remote sign post in Australia

"Hey, we can't look that bad"

of road almost ready to drive on. After so many thousand miles of working the blade lever, Doug could leave the ground behind almost as if it had been graded. This was by no means as easy as it looked, I found, when I tried it several times. I left behind holes a yard deep followed by hills as high. After my efforts I discovered it was much easier to drive through the bush alongside the cleared section.

When Doug had joined to the finished end once more, a straight-through cut-back, with the blade at an angle, made the road nearly as wide again. After grading, the road was as ready for use as we had time to make it, and the bulldozer could repeat the operation for the next stretch.

We were back and into it again at last, but we returned to the camp for the night now. The 'dozer lay silently over that first sandhill with the familiar wall of scrub in front of the blade ready for attacking next morning. Doug came back to camp with me in the Rover. Scotty could always have the grader in camp each night as it travelled faster than a truck on its own in this country. Although we had made fully a quarter of a mile of the hundred and fifty to go to the Nullarbor, it wasn't worth moving the camp to the head of the road, a thing which we mostly did every day to save the fuel in returning to a standing camp. A new road in the bush, however smooth, is extremely heavy to drive on with its loose sand and dust surface, and we found it takes half a dozen years for the sparse traffic to compound it. At the same time, the finer and more powdery the dust became before the only shower or two of rain we received fell each year, the harder and more consolidated the finished road would be, provided vehicles could be driven over it when still wet.

The next day Doug and I were off to the machine first thing and when it was ready with the big motor going, I ploughed away into the scrub ahead and shone a mirror flash from the top of the next sandhill. We had devised a system of signals with which Doug could call me if he needed something; he used the throttle lever to rev up the diesel several times. This would bring me back in the Rover through the scrub to see what was wrong, as I could hear the roar of the engine miles away in the otherwise quiet bush. Sometimes it would be a broken cable or burst hydraulic line, a mulga stake jammed into the track brake mechanism, or even only a refill of his water bag from my Rover tank that he wanted.

Once I returned to find the whole steel caterpillar track on one side of the 'dozer had flown off after the master pin holding it all on had snapped. It took us half a day to lever this back into position, using crowbars and ten ton jacks.

I couldn't signal to him, apart from sending up a different coloured flare from the signal gun, as he couldn't hear anything other than the screaming engine in front of him. Sometimes I'd hear him singing at the top of his voice competing with the motor, both of which I could clearly hear, but however loudly I shouted, he could not hear me.

This day I was flashing the mirror in the general direction of the noise of the idling 'dozer engine, and was rewarded by hearing it revved up to full pitch followed by the sounds of the crashing as it mowed down the trees. In a minute or so the crashing stopped and the machine was throttled down again. As I waited, I heard the bursts as Doug worked the throttle. When I appeared out of the mulga I didn't need to ask what he wanted after seeing the great bulldozer, its tracks turning uselessly in mid-air, balanced on top of a piled up tangle of wood, through which protruded an extra large stump. This was going to take moving, so when he saw me he shut off the engine and we walked around the mess of logs and steel, viewing it from all angles, conferring on how to even budge it. The grader and several trucks with winches might help, so back we went in the Rover.

But when we got there we discovered the grader had fractured its main beam, and if allowed to go, it might break in half, so Rex was preparing a huge steel plate to weld with the portable arc welding plant on either side of the beam. Everything else was forgotten while we all helped to cope with this latest catastrophe as we visualized the great machine lying in two separate pieces in the sandhills. After the steel plates were "fillet welded"—the name given to this kind of join—we added extra precautions by burning holes through the reinforcing with the oxy torch, and bolting it as well with great high tensile bolts carried for other parts of the machine. To find parts often meant inspecting the rest of the plant for surplus bits and pieces and robbing Peter to pay Paul.

It wasn't until the following day that we saw the 'dozer again, still perched up on the stump, when we returned, armed with the repaired grader and winch trucks. When all were joined up with steel cables, and the bulldozer engine was running, the strain was applied and the fourteen-ton giant moved enough to let its own tracks do the rest. There was always a danger, in this sort of operation, of the cable snapping under the tension, allowing one end to whip back, and I remembered hearing of an operator who was once almost decapitated by just such an accident. Luckily this didn't happen often, and after this freak incident we were soon road-making again.

When anything happens in so remote an area as that in which we worked, there is no one to call on for help but ourselves, and even old Paul came into it at times to keep the pressure on a crowbar or assist in some operation where needed. He was a true member of the bush bashers.

After a week had passed, leaving behind almost fifteen miles of new road, I received a radio message from Maralinga asking for some more surveys in connection with the new trials. It was only three hundred miles away from where we were working so I made a further detailed survey of the route of our next ten miles of road first, then guided the bulldozer over the distance with the blade lifted. This marked out the way, and left the camp with another week's work, to complete that section while I was away.

I then drove north on our new road to Vokes Hill Corner and continued east to Emu by the way we had come from the Musgraves. Then south again to Maralinga to see what was required. The survey, although detailed and urgent, was finished in a few days and the results were handed to the scientists who could proceed with their atoms. As I gave them the figures, I was told an aeroplane was making a trip to Adelaide that day and returning in a couple of days' time. They also said there was a spare seat on it if I would care to make the trip with them. This was a case where, if it had happened over the previous years, I would have thanked them and promptly returned to my camp in the desert, but now with a wife in the picture I accepted the offer readily.

Dressing up in my best set of raggy shorts kept for such occasions, and with the addition of a crushed-up but cleaner shirt, I climbed on to the aeroplane wearing not only my hobnailed boots but a pair of feetless socks as well. I left the Rover at the side of the airstrip I had located and surveyed myself years before, and knowing the camp would still be occupied with the ten miles of marked out road until I returned, I was soon looking at the maze of sandhills and scrub from the air.

Anne would be surprised when I ambled in that night in Adelaide, almost six hundred miles away, as we had not been able to see the chance of a trip for many more months. It was amazing how that morning I had been in the bush surveying, and a few days before near Vokes Hill on the road three hundred miles even farther out in the desert. It would be at the end of a nine-hundred-mile trip that I could clomp into that house I'd bought at Salisbury and probably be asked to get the steel-heeled boots off the floor.

Before taking off I left my rifle and revolver in the strong room in the security office, not knowing that upon my return the action would cause a near-tragedy.

We landed in Adelaide, and as usual when coming near the city straight from the bush, my first impulse was to go back and as soon as possible. I saw the dressed up people hurrying in all directions in cars which would be useless at Vokes Hill, heard the noise from lorries, and felt as out of place there as the Musgrave Kid would have done in the bush. Glaring lights obliterated those same stars in the sky which I so often used in finding my way about the wild outback; men and women wearing shoes which would fall to pieces in hours with the heat of the sandhills; everybody as clean and smooth as their surroundings. I stood in my crumpled rags and hobbs looking at the bustle in the airport building and was aware of the many curious looks I received from all who passed by. Hadn't they ever seen a bushman before? I supposed not as I clattered the steel heels across the shiny floor, as much in a hurry to get away as everyone else in the car waiting outside. My watch and knife pouches on my big leather belt caught on the fine upholstery and I was forced to move them around so as not to leave marks on the seats.

As we drove up to Salisbury I was glad that I hadn't been asked to remove my boots at the airport as I remembered the socks with no feet in them. I had endeavoured to keep them from rising up by tying a piece of kangaroo tail sinew on one side and passing it under my foot to attach it to the other. I thought this in itself probably looked a bit odd to these city folk.

Not being able to send a message ahead about this unforeseen opportunity for the trip, I eventually arrived at our house unexpectedly, but the sound of the boots on the concrete was just as successful in announcing my presence as any telegram would have been.

If Anne noticed my rather unironed shirt she didn't mention it. We almost had to reintroduce ourselves again. There and then we made plans for a possible trip to the desert in the future on which she could come with me to see what we were doing. Those plans kept us going and were eventually to become a reality in the form of a five months' expedition of eight thousand miles, mostly in further unexplored country, the following year.

Right now we had a couple of days before the car would pick me up at dawn to return me to the airport and Maralinga. During that time we saw a film, and in the opening scene a ragged man was shown dragging himself across the desert at the height of a sand storm. I felt at home again.

Before daylight one morning later, the car hooter advised me the transport had arrived and it seemed no time before we were airborne on our way back to the bush.

Collecting the Rover waiting at Maralinga I drove to the security office to claim the rifle and revolver before heading off via Emu back to my camp. The boys should have almost finished the ten miles and be ready for the next stretch. The firearms were placed on the table and as I collected them I touched the trigger of the rifle. Being an automatic, with an empty breech at the time of handing it over, it only needed someone to check it once for a cartridge to be levered into the firing position. As we found out, someone had looked, and released the catch, satisfied it was empty. The latch had pushed in the bullet from the magazine, and as I touched the trigger it exploded with a deafening crash in the quiet office. Everyone was equally surprised. When the shock had subsided we looked in the direction the barrel had been pointing. It was aimed at a thick stack of camp routine orders, including one warning against firearms in the area, and the bullet had ploughed into them stopping dead. The lead fell out as we opened the pile of torn paper. People were passing outside the shed. The papers had stopped the path of the bullet which would otherwise have screamed out through the aluminium walls, quite possibly hitting someone.

I made a hurried departure from Maralinga, and the several hundred miles to my camp passed quickly as I thought over and over what could have happened if it weren't for the paper work. It was the only time I'd seen office paper work come in so useful.

The first job waiting back at the camp was to try and discover a native well, plotted on an old map, to which the natives had led that previous party years before. It was the first of three and was known as Waldana, so this meant carrying out a star observation on the same night as I returned to camp, where the party was not unduly surprised to learn I'd had the trip to Adelaide. They had almost finished the mark out, and as I planned to make the road itself pass by the well for identification sake for future parties, I would have to carry on with the bushbashing ahead the next morning.

As I observed the stars I thought of how, only the night before, I had been in Salisbury, nearly a thousand miles away. The purpose of the astrofix was for my present position so that I could carry on a rough compass bearing and speedo distance to the vicinity of the plotted position of Waldana. I found it was almost south of where the road had progressed to so far and ten miles farther on.

Early next morning I again crashed off into the mulga ahead of the 'dozer working on a big sand ridge crossing and travelled the ten miles by speedo and compass. Actually I went eleven miles, as from experience I had learnt that as you travel, about a mile in ten is wasted by the twisting and turning through the trees and dunes. I must have been fortunate for once, as from the high ridge at eleven miles I noticed an unusually low depression in a valley and made for it, half a mile distant. Sure enough the six-feet-diameter hole was there at the lowest point, but of course silted into a cone shape of the same depth. Without much searching for ancient Aboriginal digging sticks or stone spear tip chippings, I turned and headed for camp before dark descended, as this had taken most of the day already.

We were now all ready to mark out a fresh course for the road, based on the discovery of the well. With the previous section completed, and the camp moved up to the end of the graded section, the 'dozer and I plunged on once more. The mulga and sandhills came as thick as ever and it took a week finally to make the last run down the last one and carry the road to within a few yards of the edge of Waldana. It was certainly the first and only time a bulldozer would be here and I couldn't help wondering what the natives who dug out the well in the first place ages before in the dead quiet of this savage country would have thought. It probably had taken them many weeks to worry out the hole with sticks to catch what little rain fell, added to a possible seepage at the bottom, whereas one or two droppings of the blade on our machine would have done the same amount of work in a minute. The grader soon appeared over the sandhill and graded its way past. This well would never elude anyone again and I could once again thank astrofixes for its rediscovery.

After an aluminium sign-plate had been erected alongside it with its map name and my astro position with the date and mileage back to anywhere, I hurried on in search of the next one shown. The camp could move on up to here now while I was away. It was always a problem to show the forward mileage on these sign-plates as the road had not yet been made, but I usually added that information on my return trip along the finished job.

Churina was the Aboriginal name for the next well to be found, and the successful discovery of Waldana in these thousands of square miles of tangled wastelands spurred me on to look for it. Repeating the same performance I set off in a south-westerly direction for the dozen or so miles I had plotted and came upon a long depression across my path in which Churina must be located. It was composed of powdery gypsum and after turning along it I followed it ten miles west to its conclusion, almost bogging at every turn of the wheel in the soft surface. As usual in these cases it was the wrong way and after retracing my tracks to where I first hit the depression, found the well only a mile the other way. The twenty wasted miles return trip was compensated by its discovery. I found much evidence of natives having been there: kangaroo skeletons, marks of fires, and digging sticks.

Back to the bulldozer again, and in several days Churina had a graded road going past it, with the camp moved to the vicinity. It was now time to search ahead for Bringyna, the next, and last well shown on the map, but this was not so easy. It was relatively close but its exact position eluded me as the sandhills grew to mountainous proportions and the mulga thicker than ever. It required another astrofix and several sun observations to get near its position, followed by two days of intensive bushbashing.

Finally the Rover dropped into a small clearing set in a horseshoe pattern of gigantic sandhills, with the usual cone shaped hole at its lowest point, and I knew I had at last found the well. It was a pleasant rest from the scrub and I could see a few hundred yards of clear instead of a wall of bush all around. I had been camping on my own for most of this job so far, only returning to the camp to mark out the next section of road which could be worked on after I headed back into the scrub again.

It gave me a high respect for the surveyor of the earlier party who had been led to these wells by the natives, that he had been able to carry out accurate enough latitude and longitude observations with his sextant to allow these points to be so well plotted. I had radio time signals and a modern precision theodolite, and my astrofixes fell on their locations exactly. Otherwise I could never have found them again.

As it was, the peaceful atmosphere of these lonely spots was disturbed by the great bulldozer and grader. I felt it was rather a pity in a way to have to do it. In this case the road could not pass by the well because of the sandhill pattern so I made a small road into it from the main access, equipped with an aluminium sign-plate on a diesel drum at the turn-off.

Being mid-October the heat was arriving in full force daily and the cabin temperatures in the Rover were often up to 130°, but I particularly wanted to finish off this road to Cook to give us a fresh start at Vokes Hill Corner the following year to carry on with our main work west to Laverton.

After Bringyna the country began to ease up for us a little as we threaded the road through a network of salt lakes after which we could remain on a straighter line to our goal on the Nullarbor Plain. One day a dust blizzard hit our little camp and stinging sand and gravel was whipped up into our faces for two days during which time our canvas awning was shredded. The fire, when we were last able to cook anything, had turned into the heat of a forge with the wind and had burnt a shovel and axe-handle which Paul couldn't save.

In another week we finally broke out on to the open plains, and as always the excitement of finishing yet another road was felt by us all. It was a weather-beaten and ragged team who carried out the last operation of the year, driving the bulldozer and equipment right back to Vokes Hill Corner along the new road. When we got there I looked along the hundred yards of road we'd started west, to see the solid wall of mulga ahead and knew what work lay ahead of us in the new year. There were five hundred miles to make, but right now I cut everyone's hair, mended Paul's teeth broken in the pocket of his shirt during the dust storm, and began the long trip to Adelaide.

As we saw the last of the heavy equipment which would be left to wait for us, I wondered what we'd be getting for a present at home after such a hard year's work, a boy or a girl.

MARALINGA

IT HAD BEEN SOME YEARS before this present work that I had gathered the original small party of bush bashers together, some from the construction camps at Maralinga where we had all been working on the atomic bomb testing programme.

During that year of 1955 there had been opportunity to observe the men under every adverse condition the bush had to offer, and two of them eventually stayed with me for seven of the following eight years. Doug Stoneham and "Scotty" Boord were plant operators there, Doug with a bulldozer and Scotty on his grader, and we went ahead of the camps surveying, and carving out the framework of roads which was to govern the layout of the site. Then when a four thousand mile project of road was needed across the unexplored parts of Central Australia for the overall trig survey access together with remote instrumentation required for the bomb trials, I had a good selection of men.

Every time I returned to Maralinga in the subsequent years, it brought back a flood of memories of those early days of survey and construction, and here we were still using all the facilities we had started ourselves for our work farther into the bush. The year before the teams had arrived in force, I had been camping on the area we'd discovered for the trials, with a small group of four men, carrying out an intensive programme of surveying, locating a site for a village and airstrip, and doing two hundred square miles of contour mapping. This last was to be used by the English scientific team in designing a set of instrumentation emplacements using my plans as a basis for their work in the office. I spent five months without stopping, gathering the material in the bush during the day and working at night until the early hours calculating results and plotting the information on a map in my tent. The map had started as a blank sheet of the best paper I could find, covering a table.

Every so often a radio message would come to my transmitter asking "how long now?" until the five months had whittled down to a fortnight. Then, after having relayed a firm date for the arrival of an aircraft to come and take the map away, we worked virtually all night as well as all day in a last superhuman effort to meet the deadline. I'd made a small airstrip next to my little camp quite capable of taking large aircraft, and when the morning arrived the aircraft engine could be heard as I was sealing the rolled map ready for sending to England. The aircraft had landed with its billowing clouds of dust behind it and stayed just long enough for a mug of tea for the crew together with some of the cook's best apple-pie.

As it took off I hoped nothing undue would happen to it on the flight south, thinking of the months of work in the form of that map with its attached lists of required survey results, all in the one large cardboard cylinder I'd brought for the purpose. We watched the speck vanish in the vast blue sky before we resumed breathing normally.

There was old "Nipper" the cook, later replaced by Mick, a huge Irishman, who made the best apple-pies we'd ever seen from a camp oven, and Ray, Bill, and Willy as chainmen. Nipper stayed for three months in the small depression we were camping in never venturing away more than a chain in any direction. Always one for a better bush yarn than anyone else had to offer, he was a hundred and forty years of age, or so we were led to imagine by the many jobs he'd had. A couple of years' shearing, a couple farming, several on the axe, and so it went, until we got to his present age, but he could keep us going with good food all the time anyway. Ray mentioned a joke he played on a friend by painting his dog white so he couldn't find it, but Nipper remembered painting *his* friend's horse white. He was always happy, until one day he had to return to Woomera.

Mick told us he'd done six months for assault and battery and was as proud as punch of the episode. We voted him the best cook we'd ever seen in a survey camp but the worst at finding his way after the day he had a spell out of camp to drive for rations to Watson siding, forty miles away, on a track we'd bulldozed from the train-line. Night time came and went but no sign of Mick, so the next day I drove off into the bush in search of him. There had been another access to the west of a salt lake, tried when we had the 'dozer, but the eastern side was the one we'd decided on for the future main tarred road. On Mick's way back, it was plain from his tracks that he'd gone off into the sandhills to the west.

Following his tracks I discovered where he had made yet another deviation indicated by the presence of a tea towel sign he'd built in the middle of the wheel ruts. Several tea towels later I topped a sandy rise to find Mick and his Land Rover at last. The Rover was sand-bogged to the mudguards in the bowl-shaped depression, showing how he had churned back and forth until most of the wheels were out of sight before giving up. Mick himself was at present fast asleep in the sunlight wrapped up in a ham-bag once rolled around the side of bacon. He could have been there forever, but at least he had plenty of food, so I slid down the sand to the bottom and tugged at his ham-bag, disturbing the clouds of flies which had gathered in the heat. The whole thing had taken on a special aroma which didn't seem to worry Mick as he opened his eyes and said a cheery "Good day." His pillow had been a bag of self-raising flour, and his face was either red or white, depending on which way he was facing. We cooked up a wonderful meal from the rations after he had stretched his great hairy body and yawned. Then I pulled him out of the hole with my Rover still outside the rim. He'd

33

dropped into this basin after dark, hopelessly lost. We cut straight across country, bushbashing to the more normal access we'd made to the camp, and he was soon installed in our depression never to move out again on his own. He smelled like a leg of ham for weeks after.

Then there was the day I discovered that the whole town of six railworkers' cottages at Watson had been moved a mile. My star observations wouldn't fit into the plotted position of the siding and after rechecking my results, found I was at a loss to know what was going on, until I mentioned it to Les, the ganger. He said he'd seen some evidence of activity along the line from his three wheel section car as he roved to and fro across his section of the line across the open Nullarbor Plain. When I drove along to the area I discovered some old concrete slabs, broken stoves, door steps minus the door or house, and on investigating further found in fact the whole town used to be there. They'd moved it all nearer to a better site for a quarry for rubble used in first making, then repairing, the line. We thought: nothing can be left lying about the Nullarbor, not even a town.

Another day, as we drove along our access road through the sandhills, we saw a strange wheeltrack over our own. It was just one, indicating a motorbike, but this couldn't be, as the whole thing at this stage had been kept secret and no one knew of the existence of our road, which had only been down a month or so anyway. Our duty was to track down the intruder and find out how he knew about our being out here in the first place. The mystery had to be solved quickly and reported to the security section down at H.Q. As we followed the erratic path of the cycle in the sand we grew more perplexed by the minute. Finally, after fifteen miles, we came upon a simmering motor-cycle leaning against a mulga tree with its rider over by a bore we had previously sunk as a try for a water supply. Of course to us he had SPY written all over him so we approached and started the interview. He straightened up and explained he was trying to get some water from the bore by lowering his billy down on a string. After advising him that the water down there was as brine as the sea we asked for his story. He said in a unique broken accent, which added to our suspicions, that he was searching for uranium indicated by his new Geiger counter and geological pick—with the makers' label still in place. He had come from Adelaide and happened to get off the train with his cycle at Watson, and then happened to ride on our new road to where he was, right at the future bomb testing site.

This was all quite disturbing, so we took particulars of his address as he told us in his accent. Then we decided to photograph him in case he "escaped," and set about contacting the security section at Woomera to handle the case. Once, as we erected the transmitter aerial, he threw his hands up in exasperation and asked the sky in general when this adventure was going to end. He was then ordered to follow us to our camp for a good meal in preference to his bag of dates and wait until the train, forty miles away, could take him to Woomera.

When we arrived in our camp he was nowhere to be found, even after the dust had settled, so we retraced our tracks in a hurry to find him broken down on the road and with a fire going to cook his tea. That night was almost his last on earth. The night shift truck on the water boring plant almost ran over him as he slept. It went off the road to miss the broken-chained motorbike still in the middle, its wheeltracks passing three inches from his head while he slept.

Next morning we loaded him and his bike on a truck and took him to Watson to meet the train travelling east to Woomera where the security was out in force to grab him. In a day or so a message came back to us thanking us for our prompt action in dealing with the matter in the bush. The man's background had been thoroughly checked with a flood of teletype and phone messages to Adelaide. The security boys there discovered he had in fact bought the geological equipment as a bone-fide amateur geologist, to search for radio-active minerals, and that he did live and was well-known at the address he'd given. They added a footnote that his strange accent was in fact Australian.

Another day we had discovered a small blow-hole in the marine limestone bordering the plain and being our first

35

experience with these, we were fascinated by the way our hats would remain suspended in mid-air over the aperture. The air blowing out did this but another time we found it tried to suck it down. After many tests we concluded the ordinary difference of air pressure throughout the day caused this phenomenon, compressing the atmosphere into the cavern in the mornings and releasing it in the afternoons. The following year when the construction parties arrived by the train-load, one white faced man staggered into camp after a heavy rain reporting he'd just seen a whale. It seemed an unusual thing to notice on the Nullarbor Plains but on questioning him we discovered it was only the water spout he'd observed. The hole had been submerged, and when the pressure was released in the afternoon the air stream out of the small surface aperture had spouted the water up as well. We managed to explain this to him before he could climb on to a train out of the area.

That same semi-flood caused so many trucks and earth-moving plant to become bogged that their introduction to Maralinga had been anything but quiet. One driver dragged himself to the time-keeper's hut at the siding, took his due pay and evacuated himself on the next train. His truck was later found almost under water with its load only showing in the middle of a lake formed in a depression. We managed to pull that out with Scotty's grader and the way he tackled it made him a future member of the bush bashers on the spot. He spent so long alone on the grader while with me that we called him "Grader Garbo."

Doug and I made an attempt to cross the waterlogged plain in my Rover to collect a film waiting at the siding to entertain the camp-stranded men at the canvas cinema, and after successfully wading the oversized flattened tyres across and back again in a nightmare trip, the film was duly shown. Everyone was expecting to see lots of eye-catching nymphs flitting across the screen, but instead it was the story about a camp of men preparing to drop an atomic bomb. I came in for a large share of good-natured growling as a result, for all my efforts.

One of the newcomers, inexperienced in the ways of the

A two-piece costume about to become a one-piece

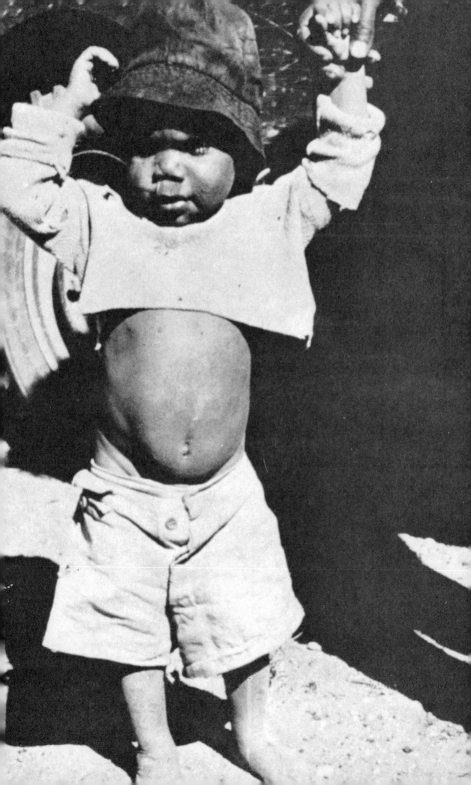

bush, had been told that when tea leaves had been dropped into a billy of boiling water, the idea was to grab the handle and swing the billy round at a great rate. The centrifugal force would settle the leaves in the water. So after he'd spent a long time making a fire and boiling the water, he threw in the leaves, took a firm grip on the handle, and began windmilling his arm furiously. Just as he got to full revs the billy parted with the handle and went flying off through the mulga, leaving him clutching the bent wire only. That unkind group of men who'd rigged the handle didn't stop laughing all through that dinner camp.

The same new chum later shot a dingo, but the bullet had only wounded the animal, so he reversed the rifle and took a mighty golf club swing at it, to put it out of its misery. The effect was achieved after contact but the greenhorn seemed amazed to observe that he was only holding the barrel of his rifle, with the butt still spinning off over the next sandhill. It had snapped off like a carrot. He was known as propellor from then on, which soon shortened to prop, which was also suitable to describe the way he mostly leaned on his shovel handle.

Another member of the camp had made a hobby of photography and would develop and print his own film in his tent at night. I returned to camp late one evening after carrying out a star observation and noticed the row of films hanging from a wire at his tent to dry. Running a torch light up and down behind them to see his results, I discovered they were all excellent but for one, all clouded over and covered with flies. I was sorry for him and next day asked him what had gone wrong with it. He looked a bit blank and took me to the row to see what I'd been talking about. This time the laugh was on me, for in the daylight he showed me a fly pest strip hanging among the films.

There was the time the chief scientist and engineer made a visit to the site in a polished city car which they had off-loaded from the train and driven across the plain along the formed road to date. When they arrived at the end of the rubble they found they were in the sandhills, with only my bulldozer section ahead over loose sand. Racing the engine

Breakaway country of the Moreton Craig Range

Mobs of wild camels still roam the Gunbarrel Highway

they plunged the car off the stones, were airborne for a yard, and fell in a heap bogged down in the sand where they stayed. With ties and waistcoats loosened they alighted while we got a near-by bulldozer to pick up a blade full of sand behind the shiny duco and push it bodily along, the car shooting ahead of the avalanche, cascading down like a surf board rider. Now driving along the smooth, tarred surface all these memories returned with all the details of expressions as clearly as if they had just happened.

I remembered a chainman I'd had who used to live under trees where he formerly worked on cattle stations in the Northern Territory, and I thought I finally had the ideal one to work with me. He refused to wear boots and ran over the salt bush prickles everywhere he went while helping with the surveys. He was also an expert axeman. Things went well until the night he appeared at my tent flaps shaking like a leaf with rage. He informed me he was going to murder Bargy and smear him all over the Nullarbor Plain. Bargy would have covered quite a proportion of it with his twenty stone but was with another gang. I asked what had happened to upset him. "Too many bosses," he yelled and I gathered he'd been asked to return to camp one night in a different truck. It didn't matter how much I told him he need not worry about the incident, he still wanted to carry on with his smearing. I could imagine it so I suggested that he could evacuate himself on the train if he so desired, a piece of advice he took as Bargy was three times his weight, and he was off that night leaving Watson and the Plain still unspread with Bargy. As he went I was sure I was losing a good man, but at the same time the thought did cross my mind that perhaps one day in the desert I might be the one to be smeared.

Finally the day had arrived to test the first nuclear device on our new site and we all gathered, huddling behind a rather too small mulga tree during the count-down. I had kept asking if we shouldn't be rather farther away, having witnessed the bombs at Emu, but the scientists in charge assured me it was safe. We would all go together, anyway, which was a very comforting thought. On the word "zero" at the end of the count, a bursting erupted from the small iron frame holding the apparatus, followed by a wild cheering from the Englishmen. The officer in charge called out in a perfect British accent "By Jove! Our inaugural bang, what ho!" and with that Maralinga was under way. The date was 17 May 1955.

Now as I drove around the settlement which would be supplying us with water, fuel, and rations for the succeeding year, everywhere I went I encountered a host of memories. The first airstrip we'd made at the site was done with a piece of railway line dropped from an aircraft which we dragged back and forth across a level section of ground behind a Land Rover and three of us had taken it in turns to construct it taking four days. A Lincoln bomber had landed safely, allowing us to breathe freely again, followed by a Bristol with Lord Penney on board. At that stage the chief of the British Atomic Weapons Research Establishment had just been knighted and when he landed he sat on a pile of old tyres while I cut his hair to the tune of the whirring movie cameras.

Not long after that inaugural bang my work there had drawn to a close and a road link of 120 miles joining the new and old sites had then been necessary. So selecting Doug and Scotty from the teams to prepare a bulldozer and grader for the job I plunged north on my own into the sandhills and mulga to survey a route. On the way I discovered a bowl-shaped rocky knob which I'd seen in the distance through my binoculars and veering my survey past it, gave it the name of Observatory Hill, fixed its latitude and longitude by the stars, and completed the recce to Emu. Pushing the Rover back through the scrub, ironing out the course to Maralinga, I collected the first party of bush bashers, whom I later called the Gunbarrel Road Construction Party, and we slowly crawled north out of Maralinga, bulldozing immediately. It was 19 August 1955 and this was the shaky start of what was to finish up as a project of four thousand miles of new roads across unexplored Central Australia.

For a few days we'd had the benefit of fresh rations from the well-stocked stores at Maralinga, but the farther into the bush we got the less the help became, until we were on our own. And that's how it was for the next eight years. We progressed to within fourteen miles of Emu when Maralinga suddenly discovered they wanted their bulldozer back and radioed to that effect, so we turned it round and drove it a hundred-odd miles south along the road we had just made. Fortunately I knew we had some new equipment waiting for us at Emu.

When our party had returned to the head of the Road, Doug and I bushbashed on the fourteen miles to our old bomb site and started up the bulldozer which had been idle for almost two years since the last bomb trials. Picking a bladeful of dirt and sticks we dozed a single track from there back towards the rest of the camp which was waiting at the head of the road, and in four days time the gap narrowed to a few yards. Then, with a cheer from the boys, the remaining section was opened up and the first road joining the two bomb sites was open for use. A great deal of survey and reconnaissance had gone into its location through that wild mulga and sandhill stretch of country and now the whole trip could be made in several hours. Turning around once more we widened out that last section, graded it, and sent a radio message to H.Q. that the sites were now linked by road.

This same road was to be our lifeline for the project ahead several years later in obtaining stores from Maralinga, the closest place to us for the next seven hundred miles.

It had been a year, as usual, crammed with work of such a large scale that each day never seemed long enough, and I always left those areas with the memories of it all, refreshed in my mind. Without all that groundwork, projects such as the one we were at present engaged upon would be almost impossible.

We drove back on this road to our plant at Vokes Hill Corner after returning to the bush for the start of the work in the new year, and the memories of Maralinga were for once overshadowed by another thought. I was now concerned with the future of not only a bulldozer . . . but also of a little girl we had named Connie Sue.

THE SERPENTINE LAKES

ONCE AGAIN WHEN WE ARRIVED BACK at Vokes Hill Corner we saw the daisies growing up through the tracks of the bulldozer. One of the huge tyres on the grader had gone down over the Christmas period. The fuel drums we'd left at an angle had the lower parts of their rims full of sand and leaves, indicating that a violent dust storm had lashed the camp while we had been away. The canvas drop-sided shelters on the 'dozer canopy were tattered to shreds. Luckily the inverted jam tins were still in place over the upright exhaust pipes of the plant, otherwise the engines would have suffered the same fate as the rims of the drums. But then lone camps always look a wreck when they have been at the mercy of the elements for any period of time.

The few yards we'd bulldozed west from the corner as a start still ended as abruptly as they had when we had left, with a wall of dense mulga scrub and tangled branches only inches ahead of the spot the blade had reached. We had almost seven hundred miles to go before this second access road of ours across Australia became a reality. Now it was even clearer to me just why it had never been done before the advent of bulldozers. There was still an enormous

41

amount of work to be done, but with that fourteen-foot blade to help we didn't feel quite so overwhelmed by the job.

My wheeltracks to Vokes Hill, six miles west, were still evident, right to the spot from where I'd walked to discover the hill itself, so we could all help in preparing the heavy machinery and equipment for the attack. The full drums could be loaded back on to the fitter's truck, tyres mended, and fuel tanks topped up. Soon the 'dozer was ready for action. I drove off into the scrub to give Doug the first signal for the year, and I waited as he trundled his machine to the pile of rubbish left at the lead out of the road. We were all pleased to come to grips once more with the country and as soon as the signal mirror flash was seen, I heard the familiar burst of life from the big diesel.

It would have taken all six of us a day to move the mountain of trees from across the path of the future road, but the 'dozer did the job in less than five minutes. On he came with the blade up, as I signalled, until we had gone a mile. Then he turned round and returned over the marked-out lane of wreckage with the lower edge of the blade skimming the surface of the ground, leaving it quite clear. On the second cut the grader came on the scene.

The following day saw the road up to and past the point where my wheeltracks ended, so I took time to erect an aluminium sign-plate: VOKES HILL 1½ MILES NORTH. This was where the astrofixes and sun observations would have to start again and my job of surveying the route ahead became once more a daily undertaking. Maps of Australia had to include this stretch of country, but the information supplied from the sketchy known facts amounted to almost nothing. It had been compiled from notes from the one or two explorers who had made expeditions the previous century, to which, later, were added comments from aircraft navigators who had noticed various obvious features as they flew over the area. About the only thing that showed was that my road would traverse the entire east-west length of the Victoria Desert, a name printed vaguely across the bare area to the immediate north of the Nullarbor Plain.

There was one awkward feature shown, however, which

I had been looking at since the earliest stage in this project, one that I knew was going to require a great deal of hard work and difficult reconnaissance to overcome; a long string of salt lakes, joined together in a north-south direction, extended for almost eighty miles squarely across our path. We were heading for this obstruction, straight through the middle, and my experience of salt lakes warned me to keep as far away from them as possible. The sandhills became higher and more confused around them and their surfaces were treacherous with a bottomless extent of soft blue mud capped with a film of white salt, deposited as the heat of the sun drew the briny moisture to the surface. As the water evaporated, the salt was left behind as a thin crust which crunched under the pressure of hobnailed boots. I had been bogged to the mudguards for days during my earlier contacts with them and was forced to camp on the edges as I chopped up dozens of mulga trees to make a wooden road back out to safety. This didn't happen more than once or twice, of course, but I had learnt the hard way that they must be avoided at all costs. I certainly was not looking forward to trying to guide a bulldozer past these Serpentine Lakes, so named after the winding pattern they form along the border.

The lakes were ninety miles away from the head of the road at this stage, but if I was going to be forced to veer the road up to forty miles to the north or south from the straight line course I would have to start the curve immediately. The main problem in this case was that the sand ridges were fifty feet high on either side of me, with only a chain or so between them as they went on and on in a westerly direction for hundreds of miles. It was like being in a groove on a gramophone record which it was almost impossible to climb out of; the groove you started in was the one you must finish in. Even the bulldozer, with its caterpillar tracks laying down a road of steel for rollers, could not drive over these ridges, but in some cases they could be attacked obliquely and the resulting road would take the form of a ramp or inclined plane crossing the ridge at an angle. As this was rarely possible it would take the whole ninety miles to by-pass this obstruction.

As it was early in the year, the heat bottled up in the sandhills and dense mulga was at its peak, being well over a hundred degrees every day, with the engines of the vehicles and heavy plant almost bursting the boiling radiators every time they were switched off. Nevertheless, it was already time for me to do a long survey reconnaissance to solve the problem of just where the Serpentine Lakes would allow the road to pass. In another day or so it would be Saturday, when a major maintenance would be carried out on the bulldozer—a regular fortnightly routine—so I planned to push on alone through the bush, to reach the lakes, and discover a way through them. In this way the overdue jobs, such as replacing broken springs and repairing broken equipment like tow bars and even old Paul's stove, could be carried out in the camp. I knew it would be useless to return until the way ahead was clear to me.

On the Friday afternoon I ploughed off west into the mulga to make a few miles before dark, and as usual in this area the camp was out of sight in a matter of yards. There was no point in looking for a breach in the sand ridges either to the left or right to cross over into the next groove or hollow because as yet I didn't know which way I would have to veer. So with this in mind, as well as the fact that I couldn't cross over the huge dunes if I tried, I drove into the sunset in the valley I had been following all along. Travelling in this direction was not so difficult, apart from the heavy mulga which had already flattened two of my tyres in the first fifteen miles. But I preferred to cope with that rather than do the impossible and change direction.

Dark came, and I stopped to mend my flat tyres, carry out a star observation for my position which I could calculate by the light of a fire when the insects made sitting in the glare of the headlights too rough to work, and roll out my swag for a sleep. Having something to eat didn't seem to be included in the programme. It was too hot. A mug of water would do.

The latitude I worked out put me almost exactly due west of the course of the already completed hundred and fifty miles of road, and the longitude told me I had fifty miles to go to reach the state border . . . and the salt lakes. As so often

44

before, when I opened my eyes on the following morning, the first thing I saw from where I lay on the ground alongside the wheel was a flat tyre. No amount of closing and reopening my eyes would make the sight go away, so I started that day off with a jack and wheel nut spanner. I couldn't sleep very well anyway with the heat and the thought of those quick-mud lakes ahead.

Soon I was again forcing that unfortunate Land Rover through the bush. Sand ridges still reared up on each side of my path, locking me between them, so there was less need to glance at the oil-bath compass above my head. Late that same afternoon as the distance between the lakes and me had diminished to less than ten miles—according to the rough speedo reading—I noticed the sandhills breaking their pattern from parallel lines as they merged together and as others came in from either side. From experience I knew that salt pans were in the vicinity. At last I was about to lock horns with the thing I'd been dreading for a year. Somehow, now I was on the verge of being able to do something about it, I felt as if a weight had been lifted from me. It was time to camp once more, and I slept soundly after the astrofix, eager to be moving at first light.

Well before the sun showed itself over the mountains of sand I was on the way to closing the gap. I had the feeling that the ground in the valley was rising. As the Rover reached the crest of the rise I saw for the first time the Serpentine Lakes spread out in front as far as I could see to the right and left. The white salt pans glistened as the sun, which had at last arrived on the scene for the day, shone down on them, and I noticed that although they were like a string of sausages writhing off to the north and south and out of sight, they didn't seem to be very wide. I could see the other side easily but it was as far away as the moon with the blue mud between, which I knew must be less than an inch under the white salt crust.

I also noticed another feature. Right ahead, through the windscreen, I could see a join between two huge salt pans where they converged to a narrow neck and met at a sort of tangent. It was not this that alone had caught my eye but the fact that the narrow neck was of an entirely different colour to any I had seen before. It had some bushes of samphire growing on it, and the distance across was about a hundred and fifty yards. If only this was solid. But it was altogether too much to expect or hope for. Nevertheless it was worth looking into.

As I eased the Rover down the last slope I had a shrewd idea that this was the first motor vehicle ever to show its radiator to these lakes. I stopped well short of the edge of the level white-capped mud, and with a geological hammer in hand I walked over the remaining distance and on to this raised narrow neck, expecting to sink to the tops of my hobbs in mud. Surprisingly I remained on the surface. I ventured farther out with the same result. Bearing in mind that perhaps I was not quite as heavy as the bulldozer, I began to feel a little encouraged and proceeded to dig a hole with the geological pick still expecting to reach the mud under what I thought was a thin surface crust. Again no mud after the hole was two feet deep. Unconvinced after past experiences, I walked the ten or so yards towards the white and slightly lower surface of the salt. I promptly sank through the upper layer at the first step until my boots were ankle deep in the sticky mud. My feet came out all right after a hard tug, but the boots stayed right where they were, held by the gluey suction and out of sight as the mud gently closed over them. Recovering them was quite a messy business involving levering them out with the point of the pick after first locating them. The overall effect resembled a large pear shaped knob of mud beginning at my elbow and terminating at the boot.

As I looked back at the narrow neck I visualized the twenty-six-ton bulldozer gradually sinking out of sight about eight hundred miles from any help, and I plodded back to the Rover to wash away the evidence. When I was at last able to put the boots back on I turned the Rover to the north and keeping high out of reach of the lakes followed them laboriously for twenty miles without finding even the smallest break. Just as I was about to turn and try my luck to the south of the narrow neck I noticed a stony outcrop in the distance. Reaching it, I found I could drive west over it twenty feet higher than the expanse of salt on either side. Carrying on for a mile I realized that I had in fact discovered a way through. Returning to the lakes, I planned to drive in a south-easterly direction where the sand ridges would allow and eventually cut my own wheeltracks of the previous day. These could be followed back to camp and we could resume the road making. It sounded easy. . . .

It was time once more to camp, mend tyres, and observe stars. As I filled in my diary at the end of the day the date seemed somehow familiar. Of course! It was my birthday. As I lay on the ground in my swag in the scrub that night I thought of that rocky ledge between the salt and what a wonderful present it had been.

The next day was one of the hardest I'd ever spent with the intense heat, the mountains of sand I had to cross in order to get back to my camp, the flat tyres, and my constant thirst. I came across one high sand ridge that had merged into another, blocking off the valley. After a dozen or so attempts to cross over by charging it, retracing my tracks, and repeating the performance I was about to give it up when the radiator hose blew off and the engine jammed solid at the top of one of the runs. When I jumped out with a fire extinguisher the first thing I saw was one completely flat tyre as well as the other slack three which I had deflated to help in the sand. All this was not very different from what I'd expected from the beginning of this job when I'd first taken an active interest in the shape of those Serpentine Lakes. I opened the red hot bonnet of the engine to be confronted by volumes of steam. Nothing could be touched until it cooled a little so I began the salvage operations by mending the tyre.

Jacking up the Rover at this steep angle halfway up a sandhill was not as easy as it had appeared at first, and after the wheel was off and before I had time to put the other in its place, the vehicle slipped off the jack, leaving the axle buried in the sand. This definitely wasn't my day. But, eventually, the Rover stood on its own four wheels. The final blow came when I discovered it was not the heat alone which had burst the radiator hose but the water drain plug under it had been snapped off in the bush and had let the water out to a point where it seized the engine. With a piece of green mulga wood and the razor sharp survey axe the hole could be plugged in place of the broken tap and by this time everything had cooled enough for the hosing to be replaced. I put the crank handle through the hole in the specially reinforced steel bumper bar and tried to turn the engine over and after summoning my remaining strength gave it a mighty twist. It turned easily, leaving me on my back in the sand; the engine had locked not from loss of oil but because of excessive heat which had now diminished. In no time I had the radiator filled with the hot water out of the tank and the engine going at several touches of the button. I silently thanked the Rover factory and backed off down the ridge to keep trying. Each charge consolidated the wheel tracks and gained me several inches until I was over that hurdle. Dozens more followed until I firmly decided against constructing the road in this direction, and it would mean staying with the original groove I'd started in order to reach the lakes. When the actual road had progressed to the point where I'd left the Rover to walk on to the narrow neck, I could swing the direction north alongside the lakes to the rocky ledge.

At the same time I couldn't help thinking of that narrow neck where I hadn't actually broken the surface. Still I could sort out all that when the time came. I had one definite crossing to go on and the satisfaction of knowing that it was impossible to veer off the road before I reached that crossing. When we had arrived at the lakes, complete with a road, I would investigate to the south of the neck in case a crossing showed itself closer than the twenty or so miles the other way.

By mid-afternoon I was relieved to see, as I slid the Rover down in a cascade of sand, that it was the last of the sandhills. My own wheel tracks from two days before were in front of me. By the way I'd come it had been a nightmare of a trip . . . from the ledge . . . but that was the only way to find out.

Following my tracks back east for the sixty odd miles to the camp at the head of the road was like child's play, and by lunch time on the following day I emerged from the bush to the graded end of the road. As usual Doug ambled over to see how I'd got on and Paul put a billy on the fire. Rex and Scotty were still at the machines and thinking of lunch made me realize I hadn't eaten anything for almost two days. The great heat and thirst had made any thought of eating disappear completely but now, at last, I could get out of that inferno of a cabin and inform the group what lay ahead for us. From my last astrofix and subsequent speedo readings I could add that I'd crossed over the border into Western Australia on the trip. I couldn't really say it felt any different from South Australia but conceded I was sure it was a very good state.

As we started up the 'dozer after dinner to get on with the road I climbed back into the Rover feeling after the last few days that I'd aged a year. In figures, I suppose I really had.

CROSSING THE BORDER

A LITTLE LESS THAN A MONTH LATER the road, together with our little camp, was within a mile or so of the Serpentines, and it was time once again to begin planning the course of action needed to negotiate them.

In this confined area of heavy mulga surrounded by sand ridges, the flies stayed with us all the time in their clouds, and as we approached the open lakes they seemed to increase in size and density. At least they turned in about the same time as we did, but as they slept, the night insects and moths took over, almost obliterating any lamp which was alight. But we were always grateful for the complete absence of mosquitoes (no suitable breeding grounds), and could sleep in what peace the heat would allow.

As we marked out the remaining mile with the 'dozer blade raised, I remembered how I'd been bogged down on the previous trip at the last rise in a hill of fine white powdery gypsum, so I guided the heavy machine around the spot. At last it stood where my Rover had been when I'd walked to inspect the narrow neck, and now Doug and I walked out on to the neck. The hole I'd dug with the pick was still two feet deep indicating that no mud had seeped into it, so with the comforting thought that the bulldozer was at hand I decided to attempt a crossing in the Rover. I knew that in the event of it beginning to sink into the mud, the 'dozer with its long winch cables could pull it back out as if it were a feather.

As I drove on down to this neck of different-coloured ground, I knew I would not have dared to attempt this on my own before. If I succeeded it could mean the saving of a twenty-mile detour up to the rock ledge, compared to the hundred and fifty yards across it. Had I been caught up in another valley between the parallel sand ridges starting a hundred miles away I might never have seen it.

With the door open so I could lean out to see how the ground reacted to the wheeltracks, I carefully and very slowly allowed the front wheels to venture out on to the neck. They remained on the surface, so I kept going until the rear wheels were also out on to it. The neck was now supporting the entire weight of the Rover. On we went, Doug walking alongside, until we'd reached the half-way mark. Not daring to stop, I let the vehicle crawl the remainder of the distance until it lumbered up off the crossing on to the sand bank and out of danger. Only then could I bring myself to stop. I climbed out to walk back over to see more closely the wheel tracks I'd left. Although we had some long tow ropes I had wondered if we had enough to reach across from the 'dozer to the far side if that was where the Rover sank, but that worry had vanished. As we walked we could hear the diesel engine on the twenty-six ton machine idling over on the opposite side and we knew we would give this narrow neck the ultimate test by driving the caterpillar out on to it. We remembered the saying about "nothing ventured, nothing gained," hoping it wouldn't be a case of "something ventured." If necessary, we could link the three trucks on to the grader, and the 'dozer might then be able to extricate itself on its own winch power control unit joined to them.

Before attempting this latest manoeuvre I decided to play safe by driving the Rover back over to the camp side of the crossing in case the 'dozer might be helplessly blocking the way later on. I turned the Rover around and retraced my tracks, as before they were left only an inch or so deep. It was with much more confidence that I watched the great steel tracks crawl towards the edge. A lot depended on our success and it was exciting to see the leading track rollers make their start. Doug was ready to make a hurried stop and reverse out of it at the first sign of disaster, and when the machine was half on the neck and half on the bank, we reversed off for an examination.

All that weight hadn't made much more impression than the Rover so we resumed the slow onslaught until the whole twenty-one tons of machine with its five-ton blade was being supported quite clear of the bank. It was incredible.

Now we had to carry on either until we became properly bogged or made it across to the far bank, so we let the caterpillar have its head. I walked alongside this time watching the effect as each steel plate laid itself down on the surface in turn. I was so intent on the operation that before I knew it we were ascending off the "bridge" up on to the raised sand bank on the western side of the Lakes.

It was a moment of jubilation. Without further ceremony the 'dozer spun around on its own tracks as Doug locked one side and continued right back on to the neck. At the other bank he lowered the blade which we'd kept up throughout and carved off the sharp part of the leading edge of the bank and carried on up to the raised section. If the join between the two salt lakes on either side could hold that weight it could hold up anything likely to come along in the future, so the 'dozer carried on back over the last mile of mark out, with the blade again skimming the surface clean from the wreckage of branches and mulga stumps.

After I watched him go I looked back at the crossing, my thoughts turning to a month before when I had crept out on to it alone, grasping my geological hammer. Needless to say I've never seen that rocky ledge again.

While the last mile was being opened up and graded, I once more drove across the lakes without hesitation as if it were an everyday occurrence and continued west to see what lay beyond. As yet I hadn't been more than a few yards clear of them on the west, and according to the speedo reading from the spot I'd marked as the last astrofix on my lone recce, the border between the States should be within only half a mile of them.

As no further saltlake activity showed itself as an obstacle in the following half dozen miles, I returned and selected a spot alongside the wheeltracks near the lakes where I would carry out a full-scale astronomical observation for latitude and longitude. From it I could compute just where the actual border lay in relation to the observation point, and later I could put up an empty diesel drum with an aluminium sign plate telling future passers-by which state they were in, mileages, and the current date. Being nearly four hundred miles west of the Alice Springs road, where we had started from in the first instance, it put this point almost halfway to Laverton, our ultimate destination. Give or take half a hundred miles, the road was to be close to a thousand miles throughout its total length.

By the time I returned to the crossing the second cut had been finished. The grader had already caught up, and this was the next heaviest piece of equipment that would have to cross. We watched as Scotty not only drove it across but dipped the corner of the blade to cut a shallow gutter alongside the existing tracks. The day was almost over, so after telling Paul I wouldn't be in for tea I went to the site for my star observation to set up the theodolite so as not to waste that night. The stop watches, aerial for the radio time signals, the field books, and the shovel for holding up the instrument battery box were all in place before I had a mug of water and some bread covered in jam which Paul had given me.

I began observing stars as soon as it was completely dark and worked constantly until midnight. As we needed the final results by next morning when we'd have the bulldozer up to this point, I sat on a camp sheet in the glare from the headlights of the Rover and began the calculations as soon as all the instruments were packed safely away. The hordes of moths and insects soon made me drag my "desk" farther from the lamps, and as they increased in numbers so I moved until I could barely see to work. At that stage I was forced to put up with them and as I opened and shut almanacs and books of tables, I had to empty off the insects before reclosing them. A constant brushing action kept them at bay until well before five o'clock in the morning when I triumphantly arrived at the final result in the latitude S. 28° 30′ 40″ and longitude E. 129° 00′ 03″. This informed me exactly where I was on the face of the earth. I was very happy to see that I was only eighty-five yards on the South Australian side of the border between the states. But we could measure that in the morning, or rather in several hours' time as dawn was already showing away to the east over the sandhills. This point was a hundred and ten miles west of Vokes Hill Corner or just over a hundred miles west of Vokes Hill itself. I couldn't see much point in unrolling my swag as tired as I was becoming so I folded up the "desk" and returned over the lakes to the camp on the other side. I was feeling pleased with everything and this amply compensated for the night without sleep and the inconvenience of the moth-ridden "office."

Paul was already up with a fire going, so we sat by it quietly yarning until the others, driven out of their swags by the energetic, early rising flies, slowly appeared on the scene. I could then begin stamping out an appropriate sign-plate on another 9 x 18″ sheet of aluminium to bolt to the drum sign we would be erecting on the border that morning. I wasn't prepared to make so much noise hammering before the arrival of the men as it would be difficult to concentrate on what I was doing and dodge flying hobnailed boots at the same time.

After breakfast the 'dozer pilot-motor began its ear-shattering noise out of the short unsilenced pipe, and in a minute or so the big diesel took over. Suspicious to the last we saw the grader safely across the lakes again before taking the 'dozer on to it. We explained to the rest of the camp that when they approached it they must carry on over, and if they got into trouble they must wait for us to drag them clear.

We continued on with the mark out until reaching the site of my astronomical station where we stopped to measure the eighty-five yards west to a spot that would agree with the actual longitude value of the border. It came on a nice flat

54

stretch of salt-bush and we marked out to be well past it, turned, and finished off the road to the lake's edge. On the way back we made a right-angled cut with the 'dozer for a chain along the border to the north and south of the road to show up on any possible air photograph just where the border lay across the "main" road. It might help future map makers to identify on the survey photo exactly where they were and the resulting map compilation would be made easier.

At the intersection of the two cuts we placed an empty diesel drum, filled it with sand, and bolted the aluminium to a raised-up flap of the lid. The holes were "drilled" through the sheet metal with four revolver bullets fired at an inch range, and I carried bolts to fit. An old grader tyre was placed around the drum and the whole thing was painted white. It was quite an efficient, though odd, sign for all either to use or from interest to see which state they were in. Later, it proved useful when an oil prospecting company from Dallas, Texas, came over with an oil lease allowing them to search and drill test holes to the west of the border. This sign served to inform them where the eastern boundary of their lease was located in relation to the only road in the area at that time.

Meanwhile, all the trucks had negotiated the lakes uneventfully and were ready to drive on up to the head of the road to camp while we used the rest of the day pushing farther west. I still couldn't realize my good fortune at having, in the normal course of my road, happened on one of the only crossings over the whole eighty-mile stretch of the Serpentine Lakes which would support traffic, without the need to veer to the right or left at all. It seemed as if an unseen hand had put me in the right valley over a hundred miles before; the same hand that had carried me through to safety on dozens of occasions in the past.

The sandhills now became some of the worst yet, and the flies were such that you could shelter from the sun in the shade cast from the black clouds of them around your eyes and head. The mulga scrub was almost solid. I made a mental note that we were surely in the middle of one of the worst belts of country in Australia. It was not surprising that no one had ever done anything like we were doing here before, and even in our case it had taken Woomera and Maralinga to instigate the project. Still, the harder things became, the more of a challenge they presented and I wouldn't have voluntarily changed places with anyone.

Two days after leaving the border behind, the grader's transmission began to sound like peanuts being ground to pieces. The front spring in my Rover snapped right off the day after so as Quinny had left for Maralinga for his ration, water, and fuel, I contacted that base by radio and asked that he be supplied with replacements. Meanwhile the grader transmission was being dismantled by Rex and examined for what was also needed to repair it. During the radio sked I gathered that a representative from the Salisbury Transport Section was making the trip out with Quinny to make on-the-spot reports on the serviceability of the trucks and modifications we'd done in the workshops, and therefore he would be returning with the supply truck.

According to a sun observation I had calculated when we were almost fifty miles into Western Australia, I saw that we were still within a mile or so due west of the spot where we had been almost two hundred miles back. It showed with what amazing accuracy the sand ridges had been laid down in the first place in the geological ages past, and indicated what a small speck our camp would have appeared from the maker's viewpoint, nestling as it did at the end of a long spider-web stretch of new road with the untouched bush ahead.

Late in the afternoon we heard the drone of Quinny's truck as it laboured along on its last lap of the trip out from Maralinga. Soon after it dragged itself into the camp and I recognized "Wig" as he was known in the workshops, struggling out of the cabin on to the road. Quinny gave his usual cheery "Good day" as he came over to sit by the fire while Paul's billy boiled for a mug of tea, and eventually Wig laboriously straightened up as though he needed oiling.

"When you come for a trip with Quinny to your camp," he said, "you don't eat, you don't sleep, you don't even stop until you get there." He had been hoping to have a spell around midnight the evening before for refuelling, but hunger and the heat of the cabin had apparently made him forget that his workshop had supplied us with hundred-gallon petrol tanks. He staggered over to our table and flopped down as Paul gave him a good tea. He then made, by torchlight, the necessary examinations so he wouldn't have to spend one hour longer in the bush the next day than he needed. I still hear about his epic journey from him whenever we meet.

During the following morning Quinny and Wig left our camp for Maralinga, the clouds of flies trailing off behind poor old Wig once more. I had the feeling he wouldn't volunteer for many more visits, and as if to make this certain, my Rover radio transmitter went out of order that same day. With the grader and Rover spring mended we pressed on with the road to a point where I wanted to try to ease the road to a level of a dozen miles to the north. Another detailed recce was due. The course of the road, once again, was heading towards a mass of salt lake activity. I knew from the look of them that I couldn't be so lucky a second time. Then again, as it affected a cross roads I intended to make almost two hundred miles farther along, I set off into the bush alone to discover a course to by-pass the Wanna Lakes, as the cluster was labelled.

A large job of mechanical work was now due on the bulldozer as several track rollers needed replacing and overdue oilchanging and clutch adjustments had been saved up reluctantly by Rex for this stage in proceedings which I'd anticipated since leaving the Serpentines. So leaving the standing camp at the spot where I intended to make the alteration to the course—a nice open salt-bush rise in a valley with an obvious break in the sand ridge pattern to the immediate north—I set off once again on my own for the survey.

The sandhills were terrible and the mulga as thick as it could be. The first night out I camped in among it all, thirty miles north-west from the camp. It had taken all day to cover that distance but I had some measure of success in the way the sand ridges had eased in small areas throughout their length, allowing me to drive the Rover across them. When I carried out another astrofix that night between mending the flat tyres, I was elated to see I had raised the route of the road to a latitude high enough to clear the Wanna Lakes and to permit a further trend to the west, above them. The star position also informed me that it would satisfy the future cross roads two hundred miles farther on . . . so long as there were no other difficulties ahead.

On my way back to camp I tried to iron out some of the bends by trying to return in a straight line. But as before, I found that my own lead-out tracks were the only ones I could use. Before I arrived in the camp, however, the Rover engine snuffed out and refused to start again. This developed into a full-scale job of finding the trouble after it had cooled enough to be handled, and I worked for hours on it in the heat of the sun. Forced to lay bags over the red hot mudguards to lean my shirtless tummy on while I worked, I didn't locate the cause until almost dark. After completely dismantling the fuel pump, petrol lines, tank switchover tap, and even examining the electrical system (although I knew the trouble did not lie here) I found a jammed needle valve in the carburetter.

I was back in camp again next morning, and we attacked the problem without delay, marking out the future road, only with the 'dozer blade up. We drove the whole dozen miles before turning and repeating the drive still with the blade up. That put the machine back in camp for servicing and left a lot of work ahead, all of which could be done in my absence. I had planned at this stage to make a trip to H.Q. in the Rover, eleven hundred miles away, to have a complete full-size overhaul carried out in the workshop on it.

Arrangements had been made for Anne and Connie Sue to accompany me on my trip out to the bush so they could see what the Australian desert was really like for themselves. Five nights later I was on the side of the bitumen road fifteen miles from home changing the last flat tyre for that expedition.

EVEN THE DINGOES WERE MISERABLE

AFTER I HAD LEFT THE CAMP, and before reaching Emu on the way to Adelaide, I again came to the point where another road of ours from Mount Davies, two and a half hundred miles away to the north-west, had joined on. Mount Davies is right in the north-west corner of the state of South Australia and a road from Emu to it had been required for Geiger counter readings after each atomic bomb test at Maralinga. I remembered how we had been in Central Australia at the time, so had driven all the plant and camp to Davies to make the road from that end down. It didn't have to come out exactly at Emu as long as the position of the finished road was known, so I planned to bring it south and east as far as the sandhills would permit, in such a way that it would cut the road west from where we were currently working. The point where I'd eventually come out was thirty miles from Emu and it was there I now found myself.

Stopping at the sign-post I'd erected on this junction to make a fire and warm up a tin of meat, I looked back up the road and thought of how much work went into its survey and construction. Also, as it crossed two hundred huge sand ridges in eighty of the miles from a sign I'd nailed to a

59

desert oak tree a few miles on the way, I once again agreed with myself that it travelled in its south-easterly direction through the worst country we'd ever had to handle. I had driven the Land Rover several times along the course we eventually followed, before bringing the bulldozer and camp along, and each time wondered if we could ever make a road over that nightmare stretch.

It had been several years before that I attempted my second reconnaissance survey from Mount Davies, having already carried out the first drive through from the Emu end. Bill Lloyd and I had gone to Davies after doing the survey for the layout of the buildings at the Giles meteorological station, leaving the rest of the camp and machinery to come along behind as it would take them much longer. I planned to survey the route right through to Emu, three hundred miles away, and return to guide the road through. It had sounded quite straightforward but I still thought of that hundred-mile belt of high sand ridges to be penetrated which I'd battled through previously from the other end.

As soon as we had arrived at Davies, I refuelled from the bulk petrol drums on Bill's truck and filled my water tanks to their limits. It had been raining heavily the day before and the ground was very soft and boggy but I was pleased with this as I knew that the same rain, had it been widespread as far as the sand ridges, would help to make my crossings easier. Wet sand is easy to drive on and I could get the Rover to places where it wouldn't go when dry.

A heavy fog had come down on the morning I was to leave on my own on the expedition and I couldn't see more than fifty yards, so this stopped me from going until early afternoon, after it had lifted. In driving through the bush you have to see as far as possible to steer for the better patches and I remembered how Bill came to the window of the Rover as I started off. He bundled in a handful of magazines he'd received with the last mail run, reminding me that on a trip such as I'd described, "you never can tell."

My plan was to travel south for about fifteen miles before turning south-east towards Emu, but as I drove away the engine seemed to be labouring unduly. I put that down to

60

the depth of the wheel ruts I was leaving in the soft mud. Several times I had to reverse out of an extra muddy area and this seemed also unusual, as I knew the capabilities of the vehicle in every circumstance, and I thought this wouldn't help the petrol supply I had loaded on. I had put on every available drum and worked out I should have enough for at least two hundred miles more than I could possibly need, to allow for all deviations in the route, but if this sort of going continued I wasn't so sure.

I'd only gone about twenty miles when the Rover broke through a maze of rabbit burrows and when it finally churned out of them backwards I walked back to see what had happened. The first thing which showed was a clear imprint of the treads of the front tyres left in the wet ground as far forward as they had gone. This was of course a most disturbing sight. With the four-wheel-drive engaged, a smooth groove should have been left after the front wheels had churned their way back out. There was only one explanation. The front wheels were not helping at all, meaning a broken front axle or trouble in the transfer case which operated them. This would also account for the undue labouring of the engine before in the mud, but with the wet sandhills in mind I thought I might get through, so pushed on, with the radio transmitter as a final resort also in mind. With what was left of the day I remember camping just over thirty miles from Davies. The rocky areas encountered had made the going a little easier up out of the mud. There were then only two hundred and seventy miles left to go, measured, of course, in a straight line.

The second day of the bushbashing brought some exciting results. As I stopped at a wet sandhill fifty miles farther on, I saw off to the south of my direction of travel a cluster of rocky mountains and was soon on the roof of the Rover with binoculars scanning them. They looked an unusual collection at about fifteen miles distance over bad sandhills and heavy scrub, but it was no use thinking about that or hesitating, as I knew I would get over to them somehow and very likely ease the future road right past them. This was indeed a rare find, so without further waiting I set a compass bearing for them and drove down off the sandhill. To reach them was much harder than it looked through the glass but as I neared the first of the cluster, I saw that it was made entirely of smooth rock, and in fact resembled the well known monolith of Ayers Rock.

I decided immediately that our road would pass by the base of the huge sheet of rock rearing up out of the sandhills. Such a hill would serve as an excellent point on which to establish a survey mark and at the same time it would be of great interest for future users of the road. It was probably eight or nine hundred feet high, so of course the next step was to try and climb to the top.

The other mountains were half a dozen miles farther south but I was sure they couldn't be more striking in appearance than this one, so leaving the Rover I made several attempts to scale the smooth rock faces before discovering a way up. At one stage I landed on a small ledge with a vertical wall of rock in front of me and a drop of several hundred feet behind, with the ledge not as wide as the length of my hobnailed boots. The only way out of that was to pull my bare foot out of each loose boot and let the boots fall to the bottom. I couldn't bend down for fear of overbalancing. Then I edged back the way I'd come. In this region, falling off the rock would mean I'd stay where I fell, indefinitely.

Eventually a fissure allowed me a foothold to reach the top from where I could see an endless horizon in all directions except south to the other hills. The sight which was the most exciting was a thin thread of water in a creek, glinting in the sun and winding away around the foothills for about a mile. If only that water, which would only be from the recent heavy rains, would last until after we had reached here with the road, it would be invaluable and save thousands of miles in carting it from the nearest supply hundreds of miles away. Even one return trip would amount to six hundred miles. This needed looking into closely, so I hurried back down the rock to collect my boots, get the Rover, and drive around to the water. On the way down more rock holes appeared full of water, with some spilling over and trickling down to the next. The rain had been widespread after all.

When I reached the creek I found it was four feet wide and three feet deep in a water-worn channel a mile long. There were thousands of gallons in it and as I was following it alongside the whole vehicle began to sink in a soft patch, until the sump protection plates rested squarely on the surface. Out came my axe, shovel, jack and steel jack plate, and I began chopping without even looking to see what had happened. I'd seen it all so many times before. It took dozens of lengths of mulga branches laid across each other to finally support the jack, and that was for only one wheel. It was here the absence of the front wheel drive became all too apparent as the back wheels only would turn. I was digging for hours to get the logs under the tyres and eventually camped on the spot to resume the salvaging operations the next day. It was not very often I had the pleasure of camping alongside a freshwater brook.

Another half a day saw the Rover freed from the area and on dry ground a chain away, so I continued to explore the rest on foot. The stream petered out on to a salt-bush flat, but at its mouth there was a huge rock pool overflowing with rain water, and this alone was about the size of a five thousand gallon storage tank. The road would surely pass this oasis, although I knew it to be temporary only.

It was with regret that I left it to push on towards the sandhill belt and also with the disturbing knowledge that the front wheels were definitely not helping. I had spare axles on order before leaving but they hadn't at that time arrived. The spares I always carried had been used not long before.

I'd only covered half a mile when I noticed a native carving on a dry mulga tree as I passed by. I stopped to examine and photograph it. It was in the shape of a foot long pear-drop cut into the trunk. Looking about for others, I found a similar one on another tree on the far side of the wheeltracks left by the Rover. I'd passed between the two and there was the vehicle leaning over on one side with a flat tyre already. The amazing thing about that was that when we eventually pushed the road down past the mountain and between the same two trees, I received another flat tyre within yards of the same spot. Not only that, but when the bulldozer passed between them, the steel blade lift-cable snapped one length of the machine from the carvings. After mending it and pressing on, we later returned to find the grader barely past the trees with a flat tyre spread all over the ground. It had a mulga stake protruding from it after coming to rest on the site of all the other mishaps. It was as though anything to pass between the carved trees was doomed.

Apart from some of the heaviest scrub ever which followed in the next fifty miles, the sandhills kept quiet and going was reasonable, allowing the rear-wheel-drive vehicle to keep going, but then it happened. The first of the sand ridges loomed up and being still wet, the Rover was able to cross it via a shallow saddle in its length, a feat which gave me some false hope. The ridges which followed soon made this fade and I was already beginning to plan how I was going to get out of this with a little over a hundred miles to go.

The wet ground caused by the rain had made the Rover burn up a lot more petrol than I could allow for, as it churned through the soft country leaving deep wheeltracks and it was now not only the axle which drew attention but the level of the petrol in the tanks. It fast became apparent that I couldn't make it through to Emu complete with the vehicle, but perhaps I could get within walking distance.

Then, as a final stroke, as I was trying to get over a large ridge, one of the remaining back axles snapped, which not only solved the petrol problem but left the Rover right where it was for the succeeding three weeks.

The first thing to do was put up a canvas awning to live under, out of the heavy dews and frosts at that time of the year, and build a fire. That fire never went out for weeks either. Then came the need for an astronomical observation to determine my exact latitude and longitude and transmit the information to the radio base at Maralinga and Woomera before my battery went flat. That night after the star observation it was with almost frozen hands that I packed away the theodolite and instruments, and knew I could save the calculations for the next day for once. The pages of the field-books were wet with dew anyway. So it was there that I lay down in my swag on the ground after heaping wood on the fire for the first of many nights to come.

When I shivered myself awake in the morning I saw all the crystals of ice which had formed on the canvas awning, like miniature stalactites, as the dew froze before dripping off, and also the film of white frost over my swag. Getting up and nestling the pile of wood I'd collected the night before into the still glowing embers under the pile of white ash over my fire, a blaze soon sprang up to thaw out my hands and feet. The leather hobnailed boots were like buckets of ice to put on bare ankles but in no time I warmed to the stage of being able to move without creaking. After eating a tin of stew I got out the field-book and began the calculations of the last night's observations, knowing that the meal represented the last of the stew. At this stage in the expedition, everything I ate was the last of that item of food. I had enough water as in these temperatures the engine radiator seldom required even topping up.

As soon as the calculations were finished I began calling the base communications centres armed with a latitude and longitude to transmit, telling them where a Land Rover lay stranded and asking for a possible air drop of not only axles but also some petrol. The base operator replied and repeated the information accurately, and assured me he would pass it all on to H.Q. With an arrangement to recall him at an agreed time later I switched off and made a recce of my environs to find a high spot from which to see out to the far horizons in search of any help. The sandhills stretched away to infinity, viewed from my selected vantage point, a hundred yards from my present "home," and I knew that although I hadn't seen anyone for quite a while, it would be sometime yet before I saw another face, if at all. At that time I remembered Bill at Mount Davies and how he had bundled in the handful of magazines with the remark "You never can tell." It didn't occur to me that I might know every word in them by heart before I pulled out of this one.

When the time came to contact the base I switched on and heard some other team already talking, so I waited. Half an

65

hour later I was still waiting, until they finally finished their transmission, and while discovering the base had started negotiations for the aeroplane and answering their repeated queries on my supplies of food and water, the radio transceiver began to diminish in volume until both our transmissions became unreadable. That half hour wasted that much life out of the battery so I needed to start the engine to recharge it. By this time the starter wouldn't budge the crankshaft and it required ten minutes of grinding away with the handle to get it going. In an hour the battery should have a little more current in it, but as the petrol level was fast diminishing in my last tank, the time was approaching when I would have a flat battery to put my transmissions off the air completely, and no petrol left with which to recharge it.

Getting up to my ever-present fire the following day I decided to cut my hair. This over I ate a small flour and water damper I made in the coals, after smearing it with jam, and continued with the study of Bill's magazines. Next day I started off with my first shave in a few weeks as my face was becoming quite like the surrounding spinifex clumps and just as prickly. Then came another damper, this time with a tin of sausages, after which I took the rifle and walked off into the sandhills hoping to see a rabbit, goanna, or anything that moved, to help with the rations but all I saw was a dingo which looked very miserable. He didn't even bother to lope away so I was fairly certain he'd never seen anyone before. I spoke to it in a croak as I hadn't said anything since the last radio sked two days before. We became quite firm friends in the following week and a half.

Time came for another sked and this time I gathered that a Canberra jet bomber was standing by at Woomera to fly out as soon as he had something to drop. I informed them that I still had something to eat, and switched off immediately.

Several more days of magazine study, walks with rifle, talking to the dingo, and trying to get warm at night followed and I thought at least in a month I would be able to vary the routine with another haircut. Finally it was decided at H.Q. that if several Rovers could reach me from the Emu end with a mechanic and all the parts needed, it might be possible to get into the vicinity and be guided to my position with a series of signal pistol flares which were always among my load on the Rover. They could be seen up to twenty odd miles at night so, with what power was left in the battery, we arranged a time and that distance could be narrowed with each successive evening's compass bearings.

By this time I hadn't enough petrol left to recharge the almost flat battery and as I held the microphone for the last time I saw my knuckles were showing more prominently as the food dwindled. My walks from the camp became shorter as I clutched the rifle but in this desolate area the only moving things, apart from my friend the miserable dingo, were the lightning quick bicycle lizards.

Each night at eight o'clock I would walk up to the vantage point and fire three signal flares spaced ten seconds apart, and one evening I saw an answering glow away to the east. With prismatic compass and torch I read a careful bearing to it and tried the radio once more when I returned to my lone camp. It lasted long enough to gather they had seen my flare and after an exchange of compass bearings which checked the radio flickered off for the last time.

Another day passed before I heard the sound of Rover engines in the quiet bush and began firing flares at intervals until three vehicles topped a sand ridge overlooking my camp. They had seen my fireworks display and by an extraordinary coincidence it was the 4th July. My fire was blazing and with green branches I set up a final cloud of smoke and over they came. I knew some of them but the first thing John, who was driving the lead vehicle said, as he drove alongside was, "Excuse me, but do you happen to know where Mr Beadell lives?"

My billy was boiling and we had some coffee while the mechanic was discovering he had brought the wrong parts. Everything burnable for a large area around was already used so we decided to leave the stricken Rover and return to Emu and on to Maralinga together in the other Rovers. We could get the right parts and again make the hundred-mile trip back to reclaim my survey wagon.

By the time we had done that, I knew more about the remaining section of country and saw clearly that I could never, in any case, have got through with that front broken axle. The sand ridges were just as high and numerous as they were when I had last pushed through that area on a previous expedition five years before.

When we once again had my Rover mobile, I carried on with my original road recce from where it had been interrupted. I had emerged on the track made west from Emu, and now I was boiling a billy there on my way back from the Wanna and Serpentine Lakes. As I sat by the fire the memories of that survey trip came back to me as clearly as if it had been yesterday.

Then, I had followed the same road the thirty miles into Emu. Because I had not relished the idea of retracing my tracks to Mount Davies to iron out the route for the road as I had originally intended when I left Bill there, I had made an eight-hundred-mile trip via the Alice Springs road back to Davies.

It would all have to be done again when we came to construct the road, but after such a wild sort of solo expedition I thought a few weeks' rest would give me a fresh approach.

"But you said it would be fun"—Connie's fortnightly rinse

The wild "Warburton Welcome" proved too much for Connie

WATCH OUT FOR THE BUSHIE

AT THE TIME OF THE INTERRUPTED EXPEDITION I followed the same road as I was on at present for the next two hundred miles before turning north, but right now I was on my way to Adelaide to bring my family out into this country. As I drove the remaining distance to the Alice Springs road at Mabel Creek station, I reconstructed in my mind the events of that previous return to my camp at Mount Davies.

There had been much more rain in these parts than farther out although an onlooker might have pointed out that I was not exactly in the suburbs yet, but it was still comparative civilization to me. The main road was under water in the depressions for long stretches and as I pushed the battered Rover along, each pool served to snuff out the engine as the water sprayed on to some bared wires. A round Australia car trial was in progress at the time, and as each car hurtled past I received a further coating of mud as I tried in vain to dry out the wiring. At one stage the Rover stopped for good and nothing I could do with a rag would help to dry it. The vehicle was in the middle of the road near a bend through the mulga scrub bordering it on either side. I couldn't leave it overnight. It was already eleven o'clock.

Municipal Chambers in Morgans ghost gold town

Superior native accommodation at Warburton

One of the trial cars would surely crash into it, as on and on they came, and it was impossible to push it off to one side. Then the starter button came to the rescue and crawled it out of harm's way into the black gloomy bush. It was beginning to rain again and I knew that while I lay under a piece of canvas for what was left of the night, the warmth of the engine would dry it out by morning and allow me to continue back to my camp. I'd been away for much longer than I had expected to be when I left Bill at Davies.

All through the night the cars in the trial came hammering along, each spraying me with mud-coated stones as they careered around the bend in the road, and I remembered thinking how quiet this road was normally. There used to be a car or two a week. I would have been better off, I felt, still stranded in the quietness of the sandhills three hundred odd miles to the west of my present noisy, mud-sprayed bedroom. I learnt later than one of the competitors in that trial was known to me and I made a mental note to talk to him about that night, realizing of course that he didn't know it was me he helped to bury.

The next day the engine fired and I was off again but the strain had been too great for the starter-motor bushings so that I had to grind away with the crank handle at each future restarting. I could fix that back in the camp after beginning our operations on the new road. Three nights later saw my mud-covered Rover stop at the camp at Davies and Bill was the first to come over. It seemed ages since I had left him there but now the bulldozer, grader, and the rest of the equipment had joined him and we lost no time in getting over to the fire where the rest were, to thaw out. Paul as usual had a billy on. It was a pleasant change to have some of his good food to eat. I hoped it would add a little more covering to my bony knuckles.

I told the boys about the mysterious carved trees near the wonderful rock hill with its river—which they didn't believe—and the nightmare sandhill belt—which they did. The next morning we were into it, bulldozing first thing, fresh from the enforced lull in the proceedings. At least the camp was fresh, and I could recover from my survey expedition as we went. Scotty stopped the grader during that first day to wind up his watch which he accidentally left on a tyre of his machine before driving off to catch up with the 'dozer. When he remembered it we went back to help him find it, which we did, but we found that after an eleven-ton machine has driven over a pocket watch it takes on the appearance of an omelette.

From my astrofixes on the recce I knew I could safely stay with my own wheeltracks for the first sixty miles, then the direction would start veering the road to pass the rocky hill with its "river." Little goals like that to be reached along the way made the overall project seem not so impossible. Nevertheless, I came in for much friendly teasing about my mythical oasis.

The nights were freezing and a layer of frost covered the shaded parts of the wheeltracks until mid-morning, while the water in the tank taps froze to solid ice. We chose our camps each day in areas where plenty of dry mulga trees were to be had, and as Doug bulldozed the small clearing, he would knock over a dozen or so with the blade and heap them up for our campfire. Those fires were so big each night that we couldn't get close enough to them to feel warm. We were forced to stand a long way off, roasting on one side and freezing on the other. The natives and their microscopic "Abo fires" were much more sensible.

One afternoon when we arrived back at the camp we found Paul in a great state of shock and asked him what was the matter. It seems he went for a walk up a near-by stony rise to view the horizons while some tea was cooking and assured us he had almost trod on a crocodile which had bared its teeth as it reared up at him before racing off over the rocks. Paul had lost no time in returning to the camp and shut himself in the safety of his truck cabin. Actually it must have been a large-sized goanna which grows to half a dozen feet, as thick as a man's leg.

Then came a series of mechanical mishaps to the trucks where the supply vehicle lost its clutch as the plates ceased to grip and the fitter's truck became useless after the engine head cracked. This meant a radio message to H.Q. to have some new parts, which we didn't usually carry, sent out. They mentioned that a plane was due to land at Davies in several weeks' time and that parts would be on board. The two trucks had to be towed by the grader for the period until I made the trip back for them in the Rover along the road we had just made.

The usual yearly art work came due on one of those weekends as I drew the Christmas cards for the stores at Woomera. Sitting on my swag with a piece of wood from a tea chest for a desk, I designed and drew the cards and took them back in time to post on the plane from Davies to Woomera, protecting them by cutting the bottom and top out of a series of evaporated milk tins. Soldering these together made a strong tube to transport the pictures from which thousands of cards could be reproduced.

I'd had enough "office work" after that and soon the bulk of my stone hill came into view as we progressed with the road. Leaving my original wheeltracks I re-surveyed the route to the hill, and as we neared it the teasing became less and less as they saw it was going to be quite an impressive sight after all. Eventually one night saw us camped, complete with the new road, within a stone's throw of its base and I remembered how it had been the last time I'd been there, camping on my own in the mud alongside a hopelessly bogged Land Rover. Little did I know that the bulldozer itself would be in the same situation the next day.

I had been in front with a mirror flashing for direction when I saw the whole top covering of the diesel motor in view. Usually I had only had a front view of the blade so I went back to investigate. The whole front of the machine had sunk into a softer patch made wet by the quick run-off of the rains from the rock face, and the blade was lost to view in the mud. At first glance it looked as if that was where this twenty odd ton giant would remain, but this couldn't be as we still had over two hundred miles of road to make. Doug and I returned in my Rover to fetch the grader and the rest of the trucks, to lend a few pounds in helping to pull it out backwards after chopping piles of logs to feed in under the tracks. When we reached the grader it was only to find it, too, was stuck in mud up to its engine with Scotty on his way to fetch the 'dozer! It took two days to extricate the machines and I was quite pleased at our even being able to, after which we all proceeded with much caution until free of my hill. We did manage to make a loop road off the main access into the large rock pool which was still full as was the "river." It was at this point we again passed between the two carved trees when all the mishaps occurred to the equipment. I had already made quite a story of the haunted trees in addition to the oasis but even the camp of hardened bush bashers became superstitious after that.

There was a point on the maps shown as Coffin Hill, named by some expedition in the previous century, and apart from my astrofixes, the sight of that long box-like rock outcrop above the sandhills told us we were passing it. A radio message had come from H.Q. saying a suitable site for a mobile meteorological station by the new access road was required for the atomic trials at Maralinga, in an area near Coffin Hill, so we cleared a large square of ground on a rise alongside the road. From this square, Coffin Hill could be seen silhouetted against the skyline to the west, and we embellished the site with a large post complete with aluminium sign-plate giving its latitude and longitude. It was near enough halfway from Davies to Emu.

Forty miles further on brought us to the beginning of the terror stretch of sand ridges, a hundred and eighty miles south-east of Mount Davies, and after crossing the first two another message came from H.Q. Arrangements were being made to show the head British atomic scientist, Sir William Penney (now Lord Penney), the station at Giles, a project which also involved me, so leaving the 'dozer, grader, and surplus equipment at the head of the road, we all returned to Mulga Park, planning to finish the road later. By then it was becoming warmer and in fact it wasn't until the following winter that we again resumed the road and attacked the sandhills. In the intervening time we were to witness an atomic trial at Maralinga and build a better airstrip at Giles.

While at Mulga Park waiting for other members of the

party who were arranging the trip with Sir William, the cattle man, Ted Fogarty, and I decided to do some advanced cooking on his bachelor stove at the lone homestead. One item we tried to make was a jam sponge roll which tasted terrible with a filling of marmalade, the only jam at hand. We had heard you have to make a big, flat, thin cake and roll it up in a towel before smearing it with jam. Just as it was finished we heard a vehicle approaching and looked out to see a cloud of dust. The same thought came to both of us at once. It had taken hours to make and the visitors would eat it all in a minute, so we planned on hiding it, but in fact all we hid was the towel and shared the cake out. The towel hadn't exactly the appearance of just being laundered. Even so the visitors who turned out to be the party from H.Q. tried not to comment on the marmalade.

On the morning before we left Mulga Park again for Davies to meet Sir William's plane, we walked out of the homestead to find the station cat lying dead on the doorstep. Wondering what had killed it, we soon discovered a small poisonous snake lying several yards away with its head chewed off. In the fight which must have taken place the snake had administered one last bite resulting in their killing each other.

The scientists were keen to include my oasis in their trip, after the glowing description I had given them of it, but there wasn't time as the next bomb trial was due. After a fortnight of levering them in and out of their sleeping bags— either the bags were exceptionally small, or the scientists large—they flew back to Maralinga.

Our next project as a result of their trip was to construct at Giles a much more usable airstrip than the bare, graded clearing which we originally made for the station. It had served in dry weather only, but as the importance of Giles would grow, so should the facilities, and the Emu road then took second priority. As two of us drove down our new road from Davies for the grader, the rest of the camp again returned to Giles to prepare for the job. At the head of the road where the 'dozer and grader waited for us, a hundred and eighty miles from Davies, Rex and I camped on our old area to

74

service the machine before driving it the three hundred miles back to Giles. During the night I heard Rex moving about and saw the flash of his torch as he dragged his swag along the ground. Things were quiet for a while, then the dragging and flashing resumed until he pulled all his things up on to the seat on the grader and slept huddled up on that. As I was wondering what was going on I felt something creeping over my ear and brushed it off. That was the start. In a matter of minutes I was on the roof of the Rover with my swag, leaving the swarms of black ants to have the ground to themselves.

After three months the airstrip was completed and we could at last push on with the road to Emu. The sandhills proved just as hard to make a road through as we expected, so much so that in the next hundred or so miles we considered calling our camp the "Corkscrew Road Construction Party." Then came the day when surveying ahead of the bulldozer, I broke through on to the road from Emu and within a week we had opened up a new access road north-west across South Australia to the point where three states met near Davies.

There was no time to be lost as more work was urgently needed while we were in the vicinity with the grader. Three hundred miles was known as "the vicinity" and several airstrips had required grading at instrumentation points, enabling quick access by plane during the present series of atomic trials. We all carried on to Emu for the unending servicing of the plant and continued on with the grader, leaving the bulldozer to be driven the hundred and fifty miles south to Maralinga along another of our recently made roads.

I remembered now as I drove through the Emu ghost camp how at that time we had constructed our home-made "atomic" bomb with left-overs at the site. While servicing the machinery we'd discovered a carton of boxes of detonators in the bush and decided they were too much of a danger to be left. We removed the phosphorous cores from dozens of old signal cartridge flares, and stacked them all up in a heap in a large open flat of salt-bush. The fitter added his contribution in the form of an old bucket, full of petrol, in the midst of the pile and an open-ended forty-four gallon diesel drum was placed over the explosives, held up on one edge by a box of detonators. The whole thing was triggered off by a rifle aimed at the detonators from behind the blade of the bulldozer, well out of harm's way, we hoped. The second bullet must have hit the target, as an ear-splitting explosion followed immediately after the shot, sending the bottom of the drum into the sky and the multi-coloured flares showering up in all directions. With the colour-slide cameras ready we photographed the turmoil before the once flat but now basin-shaped base of the drum wafted back to earth out of the sky.

The best part of the fun was to observe the effect later, after the film was processed at Salisbury, when the alert security section asked which particular nuclear trial we'd managed to photograph in so much detail. It took months to convince them it was home-made, all revolving around a bucket of petrol.

While carrying out the regrading of the airstrip, yet another urgent request came over the radio from H.Q. We had to carry out a series of astronomical observations for latitude and longitude to the highest possible accuracy, on the special instrumentation points, alongside each one. I set up the theodolite at the first one, near a high central tower which I'd been warned was dangerous to touch, being charged with 86,000 kilo-volts, whatever they were. They told me if I came within three inches of them even, the sparks would jump out at me, so I didn't need any coaxing to steer clear of them as I observed the stars for their position in relation to the explosion sites at Maralinga many hundreds of miles away. After calculating the first one I attempted to stamp the information on a base plate of the tower and I was concentrating so much on keeping a good distance from the mast that my head brushed against a bared copper wire leading from it to a shed full of electronic equipment. After the yell had died down and the hammer and punch I'd been holding returned to earth, I smelled skin and hair burning and gingerly felt a groove on the back of my head, burnt in by the wire.

Feeling quite pleased to be alive I moved the hundred miles to the next one and again set up my "star gazin'" equipment, as Quinny called it, and carried on with the second series of observations. This time, around midnight, I was walking from the theodolite to the radio which I used for receiving the precise time signals for this work when, in the dull glow from the battery lamp, I saw something moving among the quartzite gibbers at my feet. I grabbed a torch and found it was a five-foot tableland snake gliding among the stones where I was standing. I almost dropped the stop-watch I was holding as I rose two feet into the air without even trying, while the snake was also galvanized into life, and we danced about each other in the semi-dark. I had to re-observe that particular star, after managing to kill the snake with a large rock, as I'd accidentally pressed the knob on the stop watch in the scuffle. I was getting to the stage of having enough of these instrumentation sites and was glad this was the last to be done while I was still alive.

The distance was closing steadily between Mabel Creek and me, and the memories of these recent events flooded back in quiet moments. I recalled that I had eventually completed the immediate instructions from H.Q. and had returned to Adelaide, with the head of the grader engine. This had to be machined, according to Rex, who had dismantled it in the bush for this purpose.

The page in my diary for that day reads that I drove to Adelaide with part of the grader engine, with a special note to the effect that I had actually slept in a house that night. It was something I hadn't done for ages . . .

While I waited for the grader engine to be serviced I decided to buy a new car. As it appeared next on my shopping list after the toothpaste, I went into a car show-room which Doug had recommended. A little friend named Esther, aged twelve, was with me and we asked to see some cars.

Unfortunately I was wearing my usual bush uniform of hobnailed boots with kangaroo sinew laces, old shorts with big belt holding a watch and knife pouch, with an equally old-looking khaki shirt with sleeves I'd chopped off above the elbow with my axe. The salesman in his immaculate town suit must have wondered what I intended to do, buy a car or pull a gun on him and take one. However, he showed me several models, and I pointed to one, asking if I could buy it straight away. He replied that it was indeed available, so clutching my worn and dusty leather bag which I'd made from saddle leather, I went into his office. Esther was given an armchair while I was ushered on to a wooden seat which couldn't become soiled and I asked him the price of the car. He nervously told me. I opened the bag and began heaping handfuls of bank notes on to his desk. The salesman looked almost ill. One handful included a cold chisel which clattered on to the glass almost breaking it, and I rummaged through the pile to retrieve it, telling him he couldn't have that as it was made of very good steel.

By this time all the other clerks and salesmen were peeping over the frosted glass around the office at this somewhat out of the ordinary transaction, and I felt I should complete the purchase before the police were called in. As Esther and I drove out of the showroom I noticed in the rear vision mirror the petrified group openly staring after us. . .

I was still chuckling about my memories as Mabel Creek homestead came into view. From there I continued on to Adelaide in my Rover to collect Anne and Connie Sue and take them back with me to the bush.

BACK TO WARBURTON COUNTRY

ALTHOUGH THE CAMP HAD PLENTY TO DO while I was away, so did I, and as usual the workshops had the first priority, where the battered Rover would receive its restoration in readiness for the next session of scrub bashing. The mechanics attacked it with a will, and although I knew they would find all its wounds by themselves, I always supplied a list of the things I knew about which I compiled in the bush. This would include such items as: replace brown paper gasket from the water pump, substitute a high tension lead from the coil to the distributor for the rusty fencing wire one I'd been using, and a note to the effect that a bit of leather from the tongue of my hobnailed boot was at present acting as an insulating washer near the condenser. The pieces of mulga branches wired to the springs in place of shackle plates and bolts would be obvious at first glance to even the most inexperienced, so they weren't on my list.

Then Anne and I worked on how Connie Sue could be carried to give her the least number of bruises as the vehicle battled its way over thousands of miles of spinifex and sand ridges. A section of a tea chest seemed big enough after measuring both it and its future occupant, and this lined with padding would take the worst of the jolting while still remaining intact itself. A spot could be found for the "bedroom" around the centre of gravity of the vehicle and this would help, but she was in for a lively trip.

In the week or so I'd set aside to be away from the camp there was a lot more to be done. The maps of the progress of the road needed bringing up to date, with the astrofixes of the final location to be plotted; many detailed pieces of equipment asked for by Rex had to be ordered in, as well as replacements for some of Paul's worn out cooking gear.

As usual, several requests had come from the various cattle and sheep stations to look into things for them as I passed each one, varying from repairs to their flying doctor transceivers to "first dolls" for the women. The first dolls had me puzzled for a while as I hadn't even seen their second ones, but I discovered that they really were fur stoles.

Once I had been handed a box and asked if I would be able to deliver it to the experts at the Adelaide Museum, having been informed it contained the skull of an Aboriginal dug out of a sandhill. I had placed the box on a dressing table at a place where I'd stayed while still single and had come in to collect it one day just as the lady was dusting under it with the box cradled in her arm. I asked her if she could guess what it contained and after she had made several unsuccessful attempts, I explained it was a head. She looked a little speechless until I opened it, whereupon she dropped it, turned pale, and left in the space of no more than a second. Later she told me she'd been handling it for days, dusting the box and moving it about, but from then on not only was anything of mine avoided but so was my room.

Then came the ordering of the special food for Connie and packing it in a strong box which I was to wire to the reinforced roof of the Land Rover when it was through at the workshops. Rope would not do as it would fray to pieces in the scrub and let the load fall off in the sandhills. Anne wondered just what sort of a trip this was going to be, but it was really quite routine. Then came the word that the workshops had the Rover ready, and the dust-covered spares and tools could be repacked into their compartments.

The theodolite and tripod with the rest of the astronomical instruments could then be replaced in their sponge rubber lined boxes and the oil-bath compass returned to its brass fitting above my head in the cabin. The instrument shop in H.Q. had replaced a leaky oil seal on its face and eliminated the resulting air bubble.

Then after giving Connie Sue a final rinse with limitless water we drove off into the north-west, Anne coming to see what the real outback was like, while I was simply returning to my camp. As I saw the rinsing water draining away in the bath, I thought how the same amount was all I carried to last a month in the bush.

We included the dog in the party. She quickly discovered where she was going to sit, in the middle seat with her head draped over my lap. As that was to be her kennel for five months I decided to alter the position of her head before clearing the front gate, but as we turned the first corner I gathered I was engaged upon a losing battle. She would discover for herself anyway in the sandhills, after several million quick gear changes, that perhaps somewhere else might be less disturbing to rest her head.

Two nights later saw us camping a thousand miles away at the site of the "Sundown" multi-murder scene, not very long after the event. Anne didn't exactly applaud my choosing as a camping area a place where three bodies were discovered shot to death, but it happened to be getting late and it was time to stop. As we were by our fire, a car on the main road to Alice Springs stopped when they saw the glow. This was exactly what had happened not long before, so it didn't do anything to ease the atmosphere. The people from the car had just pulled up to boil their billy after which they carried on . . . without even shooting at us once.

We stayed at Victory Downs homestead the next night where Pat Moreton met the person who had managed to convince me to be less free than she knew me to be. Pat explained that Colin, her husband, was camping by Swamp Bore, mustering, and that we must call in to his camp for Anne to be sized up once again. That night she asked her native house girls to help us with some washing and they were only too pleased as long as they could play with Connie for a while.

Victory Downs was the starting point for almost a thousand miles of road, extending across Central Australia and named in Western Australia as the Gunbarrel Highway. It was only a few years ago that we had commenced bulldozing from the front gate of the house fence, after digging out a hole in a dry creek bed which, after rain, might serve as a swimming hole for the children. The hole was still dust dry as there had been a period of a dozen years of drought.

We were off again early next morning, soon to call in on the cattle camp at Swamp Bore where Colin ambled over to inform me that I was finished completely. He had seen me camping on the ground, before graduating to a stretcher, but the sight of the mattress in the Rover was too much altogether. He proceeded to tell Anne in detail all he knew about me, until he noticed the tea chest containing Connie in the back, finishing up his spiel with the hopeless comment that he never thought he'd live to see the day. He pulled his dusty hat down over his eyes, from where he had pushed it to the back of his head as he looked into the Rover, and made clicking noises with his tongue as he walked on his high-heeled riding boots back to his horse. As we drove away on the road our party had made, I waved to him. He just sat in the saddle, sadly wagging his head. Anne was learning fast as this was to happen with everyone we were to meet in the next five months.

After returning the repaired flying doctor transceiver to Mulga Park station and stopping for another camp among the desert oaks which extended into Western Australia, we passed through our Giles weather station to camp by the Rawlinson Ranges alongside the Gunbarrel Highway. We had been on our own road since leaving Victory Downs and still had two hundred miles to go before resuming the bushbashing through the untouched country south of the Warburton Ranges native mission. The mission had an access to Laverton four hundred miles to the south-west but our plans were eventually to make a road from it to Rawlinna on the Nullarbor Plain Trans-Australian Railway line, also

400 miles away, but almost due south. It was part of the current project to complete the east-west road access from Emu to Laverton, but the first thing was to reach the camp at the head of the road where the boys must be coming to the end of the machinery servicing.

I had thought of simply driving out along the road we had just made to reach them, from Mabel Creek via Emu and the Serpentine Lakes, but decided to make use of this return trip to carry out the recce survey from the western end. I planned to push through the bush across the sandhills from Warburton, two hundred miles south, to a point where the two future roads should intersect at the Neale Junction, then turn east and travel with the sand ridges for about a hundred miles. By a series of astronomical observations and latitudes obtained from the sun, I could then arrive at the camp at the end of the road finished so far, where the boys would be waiting. I'd managed to have several radio conversations with them over the spare transceiver in the camp and I gathered they had finished the miles we had marked out with the 'dozer before I had left. They'd even had time to bulldoze more off the sandhill crossings than we usually had time for, and I was glad now of the latitude and longitude of this spot which I'd calculated from the stars when I was last there. I had done that with a view to carrying out my present plan of action, rather like navigating a ship to a pre-plotted port across the sea, but the rolling and pitching of my Rover would be caused by spinifex, sandhills, and logs in place of waves.

Being July, with the white frost again lasting in the shaded parts of the ground till mid-morning, I picked those areas for our camps where there were dry mulga trees for our huge camp fires, and at dusk, the night before reaching Warburton, we drove off the Gunbarrel Highway to a clump a hundred or so yards across the spinifex. In minutes we had a large fire going and a billy on, with Connie Sue trussed up in warm clothes to enable her to survive through the night in her tea chest. As I looked at her I couldn't help thinking of the tough little piccaninnies who simply lay down on the gravel with nothing on and slept probably equally well near the few coals which served them for a fire.

As yet there were no flat tyres to mend and no stars to be observed, but as we stood by the warmth of the fire I thought I caught a glimpse of a light away to the west, coming from the general direction of the rest of the Gunbarrel Highway. I indicated the position to Anne. It had immediately gone out, but as we probed out into the darkness with our fire behind us, it flickered on again and continued to alternate until it became steady. At this stage another appeared behind it and the sound of engines came to us. I wondered who could be driving along our road and at this time of night, 'specially in such a remote area, where a traveller couldn't hope to get anywhere even if he kept going all night.

Eventually the headlights of two vehicles grew in brightness and the revving of the motors could be heard above the clattering of their load as they negotiated the ant beds I knew only too well to be there. At last, a full hour after first seeing them, they drew alongside our camp, and like moths attracted to a lamp they stopped for a moment and drove off the road towards the glow of our huge fire. After pulling up, out clambered a man and a woman with a small child cradled in her arms, mostly hidden by the bundle of yellow blankets, and two more men from the rear vehicle. By then, of course, we had put on a billy, so I told them they were just in time for a hot mug of tea and introductions followed. Their party consisted of a geologist, his wife and baby, and another driver with a helicopter pilot as his passenger, and they had been carrying out some geological mapping, now the road was in, with the occasional aid of a helicopter. This was a ground trip for a change, and when they learned our names they immediately said they had been wanting to meet up with this elusive bush basher who had made the road. I wondered if they were going to thank me or punch me. During that day they had climbed up Mount Beadell, the hill to which the maps had lately given my name, and each aluminium sign-plate I'd nailed to blazed trees throughout the length of all our roads

"Good day! Well, what are you all gawkin' at?"—Quinny didn't let a broken radiator stop him

"There must be a way out of this—beetles can do it"—The replacement truck had a good radiator at least

bore my name. The latter served really as a sort of signature after the information on the plates so that any future traveller would know whom to blame for any inaccuracies.

The water was boiling by then, and while some had coffee, others had cocoa before the tea leaves were thrown into what was left of the water. Anne and the geologist's wife were by this time well into a discussion on babies and how each handled various situations relating to feeding and dealing with the white flags. Connie Sue was fast asleep in her tea chest. Our visitors had to use a torch to inspect her. As it was not long after tea, there was food still available in the tiny cans for Connie's sister-in-arms. The geologist was making use of this unexpected meeting to spread his maps out in our firelight among the spinifex clumps and enlist my help in locating any stony outcrops I'd encountered during the survey and construction of the road. With the helicopter pilot alongside, the sort of country could be indicated over which he would fly to reach the places beyond the final location of the road, and latitudes and longitudes were given to help with his navigation. Their fourth member, an expert mechanic, was attending to various foreign noises under his vehicle which didn't fit in with the usual set of rattles, and from time to time more dry mulga trees added to the fire.

At last, well into the night, they rolled out their swags by the fire after they had finished eating some of the fresher food we had just brought from Victory Downs and Giles, while Anne and I climbed into the Rover with Connie. I was thinking of Colin's opinion of the mattress and my "being finished" when sleep soon took over.

The heap of glowing embers didn't take much converting into warm flames as a tuft of spinifex was thrown on next morning, and we were all ready to go our separate ways after our billies were packed away. Connie didn't even seem to wonder where all the people had come from during the night.

Later in the morning, as we drove on towards Warburton mission, we were astounded to see yet another vehicle coming towards us, and as we closed the distance we pulled off the road and stopped, as did the newcomers. All this

Up to six flat tyres a day needed mending when bushbashing

heavy traffic and crowds were new to me in this area, and I said as much to them after seeing it was another family, also a geologist with wife and baby who emerged from their loaded-down truck. They also were surprised to meet the maker of these roads and another discussion followed about survey locations while the wives inspected each other's child. A fire and billy followed and we all had an early lunch camp while the yarning continued non-stop. I'd never seen so many people on the Gunbarrel Highway and was pleased it was being used for general purposes as well as our own geodetic surveys.

In the next fifty miles to the mission I prepared Anne for the usual wild Warburton welcome in store for us, which I had received each time I drove into the settlement. I knew probably all the natives there, as well as the missionaries and the white school teachers, and was always sure of a boisterous reception, but with Anne and Connie in tow it would be like a riot. A mile short of the few buildings comprising the village we stopped to refuel from the several drums of petrol I'd placed in the bush in advance of this operation months before, after which we continued on to the "arena."

If Anne had thought I was exaggerating about the reception, she would soon believe me as the natives — mostly piccaninnies — came swarming towards the Rover when we still had a quarter of a mile to go, until we were forced to stop near the first of the buildings. The noise was deafening as each one of the hundred or so yelled at the tops of their little voices, pressing their noses flat all over the windows and windscreen. The Rover rocked on its springs as they surged around and all over it, and for twenty minutes it was impossible to open any door to climb out. Anne had Connie on her lap at this stage and as she looked around at the mass of noses she sat Connie up to see also. As soon as the white baby appeared out of the rug the noise grew, and the yelling crowd turned into a frenzied turmoil of wildly gesticulating arms and legs. This proved a little awesome for Connie who rolled her wide eyes around the sea of faces and started crying. Whereas it was only yelling before, at the sight of this latest action it turned to screaming, which did nothing to ease Connie's mind, and she joined in. Was I glad to see Ken Siggs, the present missioner, easing his way through towards the vehicle. He eventually made his voice heard, and the native children relaxed their pressure on the doors as they made room for them to be opened, leaving only their nose smears on the glass. Anne was completely speechless throughout, not that anyone could have heard her if she had said anything.

When we at last stood on the ground the native children clustered around Connie to begin tugging at her hands and feet and touching her face with the result that she continued to cry lustily. All this time Ken was helping us to gain the protection of his house which we were all but forced into by the crowd who retreated to summon strength for another attack at the first opportunity.

So this was Warburton . . . and the last of the roads we were to see for the next six hundred miles of bushbashing, except for the head of our own road west of the Serpentine Lakes, which we should reach after travelling two hundred miles south and a hundred miles east. Then, after retracing the last one hundred miles and adding a further two hundred miles west, we would land up at Laverton making this second access road of ours across Australia a reality. In that six hundred miles only one hundred would be duplicated, leaving the reconnaissance for five hundred miles of new road to be done for the first time. It would all have to be done again in detail as we bulldozed our way through but I needed to discover in advance what obstructions there were to be avoided.

Mrs Siggs and Anne had a further technical conference about Connie, who was now six months old. Naturally everyone at the mission came to see the white baby whose arrival was by now common knowledge. The nursing sister offered the services of the hospital bungalow. Altogether Anne and Connie were treated like royalty.

All the native school girls offered to do any washing needed, and this was much appreciated until all the things had been hung out to dry and the clothes line broke, dumping everything into the billowy red bull-dust. A cheer went up from the natives as that gave them the opportunity to help us by rewashing them all, with the ochre dirt becoming so impregnated into the wet items as to act as a perfect dye which remained for the life of each article so treated.

After tea with Ken and his wife, the whole complement of native children put on an enthusiastic singing concert for us and went through each hymn which Anne mentioned, upon their insistence, to the full extent of their lungs. Connie, after all the activity, was fast asleep in her tea chest behind the now locked doors of the Rover, and the time was approaching when we would have to do the same.

We drove off a few miles to camp, having been asked back for breakfast before our onslaught into the bush, and as our own heavy eyelids closed I heard Anne mention something about how quiet she had thought the bush was going to be.

A MINI BUSH BASHER

At the appointed time on the following morning we appeared back at Ken's house for breakfast having already issued Connie, who was none the worse for her manhandling, with the contents of a tin of squashed apples and some powdered milk dissolved in boiling bore water. Our arrival was still causing much excitement, but all the mission work had begun at the start of the day with the children racing into the rock school house, and a proportion of older natives who lined up at the hospital bungalow for treatment.

We would be returning in the months to come, complete with our new road, from the south, so after topping up everything with petrol and water once again, we slowly drove away from the Warburton Ranges Mission, and plunged into the bush and the unknown within a few miles.

The oil-bath compass which the instrument shop at H.Q. had repaired now came into use and on a plotted bearing on an almost blank map we drove by it all day over spinifex covered sandhills and gypsum outcrops to camp thirty miles away. Gypsum is the white powdery material from which plaster of Paris is made, and driving over it is like pushing through so much flour. The area to camp was decided for us with our first mulga staked tyre which spread itself over the ground in a depression surrounded by high sand ridges; being almost dusk it came at just the right time.

As always, a fire was the first thing to get under way, followed by a billy of water, and, as Anne decided on Connie's menu from the wired-on box on the roof, I mended the tyre. To avoid wasting petrol by using the plug pump from the Rover engine, I pumped the tyre up by hand. I didn't need a pressure gauge. Four hundred and fifty pumps had been just right the thousands of times before, so it should be right once again.

The dog had already decided that my lap was not the most restful place to leave her head as the gear changes over the sandhills had to come often and when they did, speed was the key to crossing each one. If the vehicle could keep its momentum without power, it could almost reach the top of some of the dunes with the tyres down to about fifteen pounds pressure, then a lightning change to a stronger gear before it stopped often helped it over. If not, the only way was to back down on to the flat and try again, being quite sure to remain exactly in the same wheeltracks. When the ridges had grown in size, as indeed they had in some places, over a dozen attempts were needed, each one gaining only an inch or two, but if that critical gear change was missed the whole process had to be repeated.

No astrofix was needed that first night. I plotted the position of the course of the day's bushbashing from the compass and speedo distance, allowing a mile in ten for the deviations. The dog was as usual first up in the morning, racing about through the spinifex to get warm before we kicked the fire into life, melting the white frost lying about, and putting on a billy of ice. I always put a billy of water on the Rover roof the night before because at this time of the year the water tap was impossible to turn on, being frozen solid with the water in the pipes. It took until mid-morning to melt and to prevent Bonnie, our dog, from helping herself, the billy had to be put on the roof.

Connie Sue was next to stir although she was still, by virtue of her strength and size, confined to the tea chest

90

until we eased her out nearer the fire to have some powdered milk and water, with some white, mealy looking substance and sugar. Adding another flag to the ones in the plastic bucket, she soon turned in again as we got under way after eating some tinned food cooked on the hot coals.

Within seven yards of our camp we were again attacking a sandhill which had been waiting for us overnight, barring our way before a tyre went flat, and Anne commented that there were lots of sandhills here. That was just to show how very observant she was becoming already. For a change, during the day the dunes gave way to several rocky outcrops that gave more traction and were easier to negotiate, although the loose rocks at times were quite large, and several had to be levered out of the way to protect the underside of the Rover. To counteract the good effect of the more solid surface, the spinifex clumps were replaced by areas of dense mulga scrub and dry trees lying flat, blown down by the wind storms which always seemed to come along in August and September of each year. The windows of the Rover had to be shut as usual against the branches as they continually raked along either side, each taking its share of paint off and inflicting grooves in the duralium bodywork. When the flat tyres came it often meant pushing on to a spot where we could open the doors and attend to the repairs. At this stage, in these dense patches of scrub, even Anne could see the need to use wire and not rope to attach Connie's rations to the roof.

Connie lay peacefully in her padded box, unaware of it all although she must have done quite a bit of rattling around in her box. The dog thought it was wonderful fun, snapping at the branches as they slid up the rails we had put on the front for that purpose. Finally, with only another thirty miles advance to show for the whole day's travel, the country rose to a higher level, and at dusk we could see an unending skyline of mulga and sandhills south to the direction in which we were travelling. Stopping on the high, open, rocky clearing, I endeavoured to contact Scotty at our camp still over two hundred and fifty miles away. The radio aerial would work more efficiently from this position.

Although I carried as much petrol as I had been able to fit on at Warburton, I was relying on the fact that if the sandhills made the engine use it all before reaching my camp, then I would at least be close enough, based on my astronomical positions, to guide the boys to me by means of my signal flare pistol. Provided of course that I could keep in contact with them by radio, which might even mean relaying my messages via the Woomera base or Giles. Sometimes the transmissions wouldn't operate over fifty miles, while at other times perfect results could be had over five hundred.

After putting up the thirty-or-so feet of whip aerial in the holder we'd designed on the Rover, I 'gave them a call at the prearranged time, and was answered immediately by Scotty. I went on to tell him to listen for a few minutes each day at the same time. If I didn't come on, he would know we were still on the way. He asked if I had any passengers and after hearing that I had, wanted to be told in advance when he should start wearing his bow tie.

I still didn't consider an astrofix necessary as the country had not seemed to veer me too much from my direction — according to constant consultations with the compass minus its air-bubble over my head in the cabin — so I concentrated on mending the collection of flat tyres. It was shaping up to be an extra cold night but we had a good roaring fire from which to absorb as much friendly warmth as possible before making a dash for the swag on that soft mattress.

There was a steep, rocky break-away escarpment to slide the Rover down fifty feet ahead of our camp and I was glad I'd stopped when I did. It had looked a bit black in front as the headlights stabbed out into mid-air, just before stopping the night before, but this required full daylight to negotiate. Loose rocks cascaded down on either side as the Rover's tyres dislodged them and I was glad when we landed on the bottom the right way up. Connie must have been lying almost on the walls of her "bedroom" at one stage of the descent. I was not so much thinking of that but the problem of making a road back up over this wild area. I would have to carry out much detailed surveying to skirt the area with

92

the bulldozer. After all, this was only the initial reconnaissance so I plotted the region on the map I was adding to daily as we went, for future reference.

We managed to gain a full forty miles that day as the country had emerged from the first sandhill strip and opened up on to spinifex undulations bordered on the west by a rough, rocky escarpment and stony hills. The several patches of never-ending dense mulga only caused one staked tyre, and we camped that night feeling much better about everything. I left the "star-gazing" equipment where it had been since packing it in its sponge rubber lined boxes at Salisbury.

Being in an area of thick spinifex for the night's camp, I burnt a large area off first to be sure the Rover wouldn't be endangered as we lit our usual inferno. After all, we were relying on that vehicle and its contents for our lives, and we both wanted Connie to live to be an adult one day.

We were now about half-way from Warburton to where our future road intersection would be, with a hundred miles to push on farther south before turning east to the camp.

The tank tap was frozen solid as usual in the morning so on the fire went the billy of ice once again. At least there were no flies, the engine performed better than ever, and the few fresh rations left were still in good order. Apart from the fact that the mornings and nights were rather too bracing for anyone unused to them, July was certainly the time to carry out such expeditions; the days were perfect. Over my shorts and raggy shirt I was able to keep on my old army overcoat all the time, while Anne had on an assortment of pullovers covered by a rather more fashionable long coat which she'd bought in England. Connie was almost glowing with warmth all the time, and I was sure she had been issued with a built-in thermostat as nature's own means of protection.

The country waiting for us on this next day's travelling was so different that it could have been in another area altogether. It was the sort that gave bushbashing its true meaning. Mulga scrub came in solid masses, through which the Rover had to force its way literally inches at a

93

time, but surprisingly enough we did not get one staked tyre. No sooner had twenty miles of that been beaten through than one of the heaviest belts of sand ridges started to bar our way. They were piled almost on top of one another, with sometimes not more than a few yards between their bases, and as each was surmounted the next would be right there waiting. Sometimes we would be lucky to advance two or three miles in an hour's driving, and even the dog took to lying on the floor under Anne's feet. She looked at me once with an expression which could only mean she was asking how she ever got mixed up with us in the first place.

We were still in the thick of them when darkness began to fall, and just then the engine began to give out with some disturbing misses and coughing noises. That decided on the overnight stopping place and again I burnt a safe area of spinifex in the centre of which I could leave the Rover. After the fire was well established I buried myself in the engine with a torch and discovered several plug wires shorting on to the block. Breathing more easily, I rejoined them without the cracked rain covers causing it all, and the engine ran as well as Anne's sewing machine once again. By this time Connie was satisfied by more of the tins' contents, and yet another flag was placed in the bucket. I walked over to the fire and watched our tea sizzling in the frying pan. I thought how different this was to my usual trips into the unexplored areas, where I would open a tin on my own and scoop out some cold meat with a chisel to eat between the nightly jobs.

I decided that as only thirty-five miles had been gained all day, I'd plot that up still on dead reckoning by the compass and speedo, but next day would certainly require an astrofix for our final exact position. Meanwhile I made a further radio contact with Scotty and also with our base centre at Woomera. It would take the operator there much less time to move the coloured map tack to the position I gave him than it did for us to arrive there on the ground.

All next day was dragged through, fighting tooth and nail with the tangled wilderness of high sandhills and mulga, but Anne made only another of her understatements to the effect that you didn't ever seem to be getting anywhere in this country. I was able to agree without hesitation. I was becoming convinced that Connie was never going to be steady enough to even pour out a cup of tea for the rest of her life, judging by the way her box surged from side to side and back and forth in its recess. We'd wedged empty sugar bags around it but they soon became compressed.

At noon on that day, a week out from Warburton, I set up my theodolite, and while Anne booked the results I observed the sun for a latitude position to discover if we were yet on an east-west line to my previous astrofix in the camp at the head of the road. After calculating the result I was pleased to see it agreed so well with the speedo distance and that the mile in ten off for detours still worked as a reasonably reliable rule. Also, as Anne watched the operation, I was able to inform her that we were almost on the same parallel of latitude as the plotted camp at the head of the road a hundred miles away to the east. We would reach that point during the afternoon, so decided to keep to the southerly course for the rest of the day, bearing in mind the camp was at the end of the upward trend in the road which I'd put in west of the Serpentines. After the star latitude and longitude position that night it looked as if we could at last turn due east by the compass and if the camp wasn't reached in the plotted distance, then I could veer the course north-easterly to cut our existing road. The sand ridges, although we would be travelling with them instead of across them, might ease us slightly off one way or the other, and I would be able to ascertain just how far with future astro and sun fixes as we went.

We battled over the ridges for what was left of the day and camped earlier to give us time to set up the instruments for the all-important astrofix. Connie could never realize just how much we were all balancing our lives on the results of these, and as we looked at her lying contentedly in her blankets, we thought of what an out of the ordinary start she was having to her life. The photographs we were taking would be her only proof of where she had been.

The cold was intense during the observing as I couldn't have a fire anywhere near the instrument. The heat shimmer alone would make the pin points of light in the sky impossible to read angles on to. So I found I was back to booking for myself, although Anne did enter the first few for me. Luckily, driving in sandhills alone hadn't given us any flat tyres that afternoon, so as soon as the equipment was packed away I could huddle in the back of the Rover to compute the results. At first my hands were too cold to use a pencil for all that paper work and I had to get out and make a fire at last to get them working. They had, several times, refused to allow me to hold the tangent screws and clamps on the theodolite strongly enough to even turn them, and I had been forced to dry the telescope lens free from any dew and condensed breath in order to see through it. The micrometer reading tubes were in the same condition.

Eventually I came up with a south latitude of 28° 33' and an east longitude of 127° 00', not bothering about the odd seconds in this big country. A half-a-mile was ample for me to base the next day's direction upon. I saw that it put us a little south of west of the bulldozer but almost exactly west of the Serpentine Lakes crossing, and I was elated to see that we were only ninety miles, instead of a hundred, from the boys. It must have been catching as Anne was jubilant to think that we were indeed almost there.

My elation stemmed from the fact that we were nearly on our last tank of petrol and if the going remained so tough we had barely a hundred miles of travel left. That would put us within walking distance of the road if all else failed so, with the map returned to its pocket in the ceiling of the cabin, we were very quickly asleep. It had been a long, hard day.

Next night saw our lone vehicle forty miles to the east, as we didn't have to cross any sand ridges at all, and it was only the heavy scrub which slowed our progress. I had another radio talk with the camp at the arranged time and was amazed that the reception was still so good. Nothing had to be relayed from any base but I called Woomera, after informing the boys of our position and progress, to allow them again to move the coloured map tack. We were certainly giving them a lot of work lately.

One more day of the thickest scrub imaginable put us within ten miles of my camp, for although I was being forcibly eased a little off course to the right by the mountainous ridges on either side, I put up with that rather than endeavour to re-cross them. Our water was becoming quite low, but as I'd anticipated, it was lasting until we were within range of further supplies in the camp. However, the petrol gauge was showing empty. It had done the job already but might even get us a few miles farther before cutting out, for I doubted if it could carry us on to the road over the sandhills. I read another careful astrofix from the stars that night, just before black clouds appeared to cover them over completely. Luck was certainly with us. After computing the results, I radioed them down to Woomera, with a message to call up the boys and ask them to listen out every hour on the hour for five minutes. I explained that I had been forced down from my direction by the sandhills and was almost out of petrol but the camp knew what to do when called. The operator must have only received a sketchy part of my transmission, as he replied to the effect that "I understand you have been forced down in the sandhills." Anne and I couldn't help laughing and assured him we hadn't crashed in an aeroplane due to engine trouble.

We again lay in the swag on the very welcome mattress to let sleep claim us, which it did in a matter of minutes. The last comment was that we'd see what the following day would bring us.

"SCOTTY—I PRESUME"

BLACK CLOUDS HAD BLOTTED OUT the entire sky after the last evening's astrofix, and as we built up the fire, first thing next morning, we saw that they had not only persisted but were on the point of rain. It hadn't even needed the operation of opening our heavy eyelids to discover that fact, because the night had been so warm, which is always the case with cloudy weather. The covering of vapour prevents day-warmed air from rising after sunset.

We placed a billy under the tap at the back of the Rover. We had been too busy the previous evening with radio skeds, the astrofix and its calculations, and flat tyre mending to remember to leave it on the roof as usual. Not being ice for once, the water came out at once, but almost immediately dwindled to a trickle, which in turn became separate drops. I jacked the front of the vehicle up as high as possible, until a little more surged into the billy, only half filling it. We were out of water but within walking distance of the road, and it was also about to rain.

After Connie had decided she would like what water we had, fixed with powdered milk and sugar, before she frightened away all the lizards within a ten mile radius with her insistence, we soon were on our way. Relying on the bearing obtained from the star observations, we made off in a direction leading to the nearest point on our previously made road, the sand ridge on our north forcing us along the level going for a mile or so until a slight diminishing appeared. It had begun to sprinkle with rain, and this had a good effect on the loose sand, binding it together enough to allow us to cross over. As the next ridge looked like going on and on either way, maintaining its height, we tried to cross it at right angles, helped by the rain, but it was not to be. This time, as soon as the Rover's front wheels began the rise, the film of petrol in the bottom of our last tank eased to the lower corner and away from the feed pipe, which was confirmed when the engine cut out. I was able to reverse down on to the level with the starter button, and when the wisp of petrol again touched the pipe the engine fired once more. I could now drive it to a good open spot twenty yards farther back, and there it was going to stay put until more fuel could be poured into it. The dog jumped out for a run in the rain, which was almost over already, while Anne continued with her knitting. Connie was asleep and didn't even know we were out of water and petrol, and many hundreds of miles from anywhere in any direction, except the camp some seven miles away.

Although it was not a very usual situation for a nursery, I was not in the least concerned, as I knew where we were to a pencil point on the map, as well as the road and camp, and if the radio, helped by the bright signal flares, failed to summon the boys, then I could amble over to them using the prismatic compass. Anne didn't even glance up from her knitting as she sensed it was more of a game from my casual approach, so I set up the aerial, being near an even hour, and called the camp. That the Woomera communications centre had done its usual life saving job well was proved by the way Scotty replied immediately, again with surprising clarity. I advised him that as we were out of petrol we could do with some, if they had the time to spare. I told him to drive back along the road with the camp Rover for six miles exactly, then to look out for a flare to their right after he had called on the radio again.

Waiting with the radio switched to "Battery economy" I soon heard him calling again, so told him to listen for the sound of the shot over their loudspeaker. I switched it to "transmit" and fired a red ball of phosphorous high into the sky. Against the dull cloud background Scotty and Eric must have seen it, for they called in after Anne had laid her needles down and switched it to receive. They were on their way towards us and would call again for further flare directions from time to time as they wanted them. While we waited I asked Anne if she had seen the dog lately. Neither of us had, so she went off, calling to it, while I stood by with the pistol, which I used again when called upon for another check. Connie had been aroused by the firing, so I put her up on my shoulders after Scotty had finally said that judging by the last shot we seemed to be only in the next valley.

In a matter of five minutes their Rover appeared over the ridge, greatly helped by the sand tyres and rain-soaked sand, and drove on over to us. As they climbed out of their vehicle I tried to imitate Stanley and Spencer Tracy with a "Scotty — I presume," still with Connie Sue on my shoulders. They looked up and pointed out that my passenger appeared to have shrunk, which made me look about for Anne. She came over from the dunes saying she couldn't find the dog, and we started the search by trying to pick up Bonnie's tracks. At the first shot she had taken off through the wet scrub; the last we saw of her for two weeks.

After locating the tracks, we emptied several cans of petrol into my dry tank and the two of us drove off in the direction of Eric, who was following the tracks in the wet sand on foot. With Scotty and Eric taking it in turns at walking, we followed them for four miles before the tracks were lost in a maze of dry mulga and thick spinifex, so there was nothing for it but to replot where I thought we were from frequent glances at the Rover compass during the chase and re-set a course for the road. That gave us a chance to replace the half-flat tyre collected since the

100

meeting place was left, and as I drove on the bearing through the scrub with Scotty and Eric following, the rain which had restarted made us pleased Bonnie at least wouldn't go thirsty. She must have received quite a fright at that first explosion, not helped by the succeeding ones, and we sadly became resigned to the fact that we'd never see her again.

Within half a dozen miles we topped a high wet sand ridge to see the freshly bulldozed road in the valley below, and in no time we were both driving along a smoother surface. It was the first spell Anne and I had since bush-bashing from Warburton, over three hundred miles away, guided here by star latitudes and longitudes. Connie might live to maturity after all.

As we sloshed into the little camp which stood at the end of the bulldozing, where the wall of dense mulga began, Paul ambled over to say "Good afternoon ladies and gentlemen," and asked if we'd care for some tea. He'd already called in at Salisbury and knew Anne was from England.

The following day was used in filling our empty water and petrol tanks, mending flat tyres, cutting everyone's hair, washing, licking the Rover's wounds from the expedition, and eating the results of Paul's cooking. He immediately assumed the role of Connie Sue's guardian, and played endlessly with her on the table in between feeding her and getting as much orange juice into her as she could drink. Quinny took over at times from Paul but as his hands alone were nearly as big as the whole of Connie, she was often completely lost to view behind them.

We were all now situated at a point a hundred and ninety miles west of Vokes Hill, and I knew the country a hundred miles again to the west, through which the next stage of our new road must penetrate, and that would bring us to roughly the area of the future intersection. So it was that at noon the next day, which was by now fine and sunny, I observed the sun for latitude in a valley clear of obstructions to the west, where I again planned to direct the course we had been on since leaving Emu three hundred miles away to the east. We had been making a twenty mile trend

101

north-west to clear the Wanna Lakes before I returned to Salisbury a few weeks earlier.

This clearer valley was several miles farther on from the bulldozer standing waiting behind the wall of mulga, ready to plunge into it when it knew where to go, and after marking the turning point at the sun latitude station we retraced our wheeltracks to the machine.

A final topping up with petrol and water, plus some spare drums which, when empty, we would discard by our wheel-tracks, took up what was left of the day. We planned to leave once more to carry out the complete recce survey to Laverton. The idea was that while I planned the course of the whole four hundred miles of road that remained to be made to reach there, Scotty could bulldoze along my wheeltracks, in this case being aided by the high sand ridges on either side. This was a plan which could work here, and thus save time, as we also wanted to construct the further four hundred miles from Warburton south to Rawlinna, cutting our present road at right angles. I had hoped to complete this section of work in the Great Victoria Desert before Christmas, to help in the geographical location of the heavy machinery in readiness for our next year's programme.

We had only been in the camp for two days after all that had preceded it, and as Quinny and Eric returned to Mara-linga for another load of diesel fuel, we went off in the opposite direction on the next part of our survey. Scotty accompanied us as far as the 'dozer that was soon started and went crashing on its way to our sun latitude station at the first flashing of a reflecting mirror. As it approached the turning spot, as usual with its blade up for the first mark out, I carried on westerly by compass for a few hundred yards to give a further sun flash to aim for.

A conference followed there, where we were to part once again for another three weeks. We agreed on sked times for radio contact, and that our fresh wheeltracks would be the course of the road unless anything unforeseen occurred in the way of an obstruction. In that case I would advise the details over the radio, but it was now that our recent reconnaissance was to be made use of to the full. Although it passed parallel to our present valley about ten miles to the south with no major barriers encountered, I could still expect the going to be similar.

The great bulldozer turned around, dropped its blade and began the return trip to the road clearing as it went. We were on our way once more with our project.

We again ploughed into the mulga, this time driving west, and managed to gain twenty miles from where we left the "made" road before camping on a gravel rise. With the replenished rations from Paul's truck we were able to vary our diet from the previous weeks of bushbashing to such things as eggs and bacon, and even some of Paul's freshly baked bread. Connie was back on her tins of food, most of which, although full of goodness, still resembled chicken mash. She had been looked after like a princess by Paul who cooked her fresh greens and special dishes which she ate willingly, proved by the fact that once she almost fell off the table endeavouring to reach out for the proferred spoonful. We had it poised and were looking the other way at the time.

A further twenty miles on our second day out brought us to a gypsum outcrop, but being narrow, leaving a crossing nearer the sand ridge at one end available, I didn't need to even note it on our progress map. No sooner had we cleared it than clouds again appeared to black out the sun and sky and in an hour the rain was again pouring down, turning our valley into a soft boggy mess. I was then forced to leave the centre line between the ridges to drive close to the raised level of sand. Even so the wheeltracks left were four inches deep and with the engine labouring I began to think of the extra petrol being used. I would radio the camp in a few days to explain why the deep ruts were so far over to one side and ask them to keep the road more central between the sandhills. There was only a hundred yards between them and they went on as they had been for hundreds of miles so it was more than just an obvious choice of direction. It was the only one.

Darkness was upon us prematurely in another ten miles and it was altogether the most gloomy camp that could be imagined. The Rover stopped dead without any use of brakes as soon as the clutch pedal was depressed, with the lumps of built up mud slowly sagging off the wheel boxes and surging back to the slush over the tyres. The mulga was soggy and black with the rain, and as I was looking out through the windscreen I wondered how many people there were as remote and cold in this almost never-ending outback as we were. Connie wasn't minding a bit, lying there warm and contented in her tea chest, and as I was about to search for a canvas camp sheet Anne put away her knitting, yawned, and instructed me to light a fire to heat Connie's tea. It was like making a fire under a waterfall with wood pulled up out of a swamp, but in time, and helped by the camp sheet draped over me, I chopped the dry centres out of some thicker pieces of dead mulga and nursed the microscopic flame into a blaze. Eventually, with smoke tears pouring down my face to be lost in the rest of water on my sodden shirt, I was able to remove myself from over the fire, where I had been acting as a human roof, and add piles of split branches. These were followed by a dozen dead mulga trees which could be pushed over easily out of the soaking ground, and the roaring fire could withstand the rain which vaporized as it came down towards it.

The next operation was to empty out the back of the Rover to clear space over the famous mattress, allowing Anne to climb over from the front seat on to it without even opening the door. The gear from the Rover fitted on to the small folding table up out of the main stream of water and mud, and the camp sheet from my shoulders kept the rain off the top. My hobnailed boots were converted by now into large globules of mud which I left on the front floor before climbing over to transfer Connie's bedroom to its usual place on the passenger's seat.

It wasn't long before she was being given her warm rations, and at last the rain was easing. The worst part was yet to come, I knew; the next day when we would be trying to drive through the soft, boggy ground after the rain and I fell asleep thinking about shovelling out of one bog after another. I would have to keep up on the sand as far as possible as the centre of the valley was by now a bottomless quagmire. We were fifty miles west of the bulldozer, which might also have to wait until the ground dried, as the rain appeared to have been widespread from the look of the sky.

Although it was still raining, we were able to carry on the next morning but not before again deflating the tyres to their limits. Even so, the wheeltracks left were still four or five inches deep and we were on the point of becoming bogged dozens of times when forced down off the sand ridges by the scrub. By midday the clouds as well as the rain had cleared and the slow process of drying out could begin, at last. The petrol was being used up at a great rate. We had already discarded an empty drum from the roof, but the going was becoming less scrubby, and we eventually emerged into more open spinifex-covered valleys between the ridges which were still with us. At one stage we saw a large bush turkey strutting along the sand between the clumps of growth, a sight which was not uncommon during or just after rain. We could go for years in drought seasons without seeing one, but the day it rains they seem to come out of hiding.

Then a most exciting thing happened. We had progressed about eighty miles from the camp by mid-afternoon, and I was on a sharp lookout for our own wheeltracks made a week before, coming south from Warburton and just short of the camp where our astrofix told us to turn east. Then, we had travelled ninety miles in that direction to the camp and with the little bit north-westerly direction gained with the road we should be near the old tracks by now. My concern was that the rain might have obliterated them, so I took to driving only on the sort of surface which would hold the tracks made in the dry, and sure enough, just as I sensed that I recognized the lay of the country, we crossed over them. Whenever an area has been visited once, although there are hundreds of thousands of square miles of unbroken country around, you get the feeling immediately that you've been there before.

This was really something to cause me great elation as I

knew that those tracks, if followed north, would lead right back to Warburton two hundred miles away and would be roughly the course of our new road. But Anne only smiled, told me how glad she was, and returned to her knitting. At least she had faith in what I was doing, even if I did become unduly pleased when the pieces fitted together. Her approach to it was that it was what I expected anyway, although I was sure she had no idea on earth where we were, as much as I explained it all as we went, on the map I was drawing. This spot then was closer to where the intersection would be, as there was nothing to prevent the making of the road so far, and the actual cross-roads would depend on the best location of the future road to Warburton. The camp that night was vastly different from the previous one. It was starry and dry, and although extremely cold, the discovery of the wheeltracks, together with the fact that we had survived the day without a single bog, put a new light on everything.

There had been some activity farther to the west again, by some mapping survey parties from Perth who had been working towards us from Laverton and had progressed with their programme to approximately our present position. The name of the map, to the scale they were surveying, was "Neale" and they had named a base camp they had set up, Neale Junction. This was a good name also for our road intersection when it was finally made, and for once the name preceded the construction. They had the services of a helicopter and crew for much of their project and I had little doubt we would all meet very soon in the bush, as news of any kind is flashed about large areas via the transceivers. In turn they knew of our activities and progress with the road from the east and were equally confident of a meeting in due course.

Another four days of bushbashing in heavy patches broken up by open patches of spinifex, put us two hundred and sixty miles west from my camp. I had been wondering whether it was still in the very same spot as we'd left it, due to the rain. We had already contacted the camp by radio, and Scotty had mentioned he was driving the bulldozer carefully until the ground dried out, to avoid any possibility of bogging it. It left us with a good feeling that we had a small group of bushbashers who had been with me for so long that they could be relied upon to make use of their previous experiences to the full.

By now, as usual in the cold weather, most of the springs had snapped under the Rover with the use they got as it traversed the high clumps of sand knobs held by the spinifex, and I had wired several mulga logs between them and the chassis. This kept the tyres from grinding away on the mudguards, and as I attached the latest one I noticed the rear axle differential housing was leaking profusely. I informed Anne about this and she assured me she was sorry to hear it, followed by the question as to just what a differential housing was in the first place.

At least we weren't short of water but I wondered how far we were to get with the remaining petrol.

"GOODNESS—MY HAIR'S A MESS"

WE HAD LONG SINCE DISCARDED the empty petrol tins from the roof and had already eaten up the contents of the second large tank in the Rover because of the mud. The jerry cans had been poured into the front tank and were empty, but at least the tank was full as yet, and the mud had dried with the last four days of sun. Nevertheless, we still had a hundred miles to go before reaching a sandalwood cutter's alleged track out from Laverton and we might or might not make that. If we did, I could send a signal to be passed to the gold ghost town there for someone to travel out on this old track to meet us, as it was going to be a further eighty miles down to Laverton from the point where my recce would cut that track. If we did not make it, I would be able again to get within walking distance of it, and after an astrofix and radio signal via our Woomera base, go to meet any help on foot. The astrofix would tell me how far to walk and how far to request a vehicle to come out from Laverton. As long as I had things like these to rely on, it took the concern out of the expedition which was present in my mind only for Anne and Connie, but without the "star gazin'" equipment or radio, I would have approached it all in a completely different manner.

The country was opening up as far as the dense mulga was concerned, now we were nearing a point four hundred miles west of the border at the Serpentine Lakes, and even the sand ridges were diminishing at last. We had been battling along in between them without a break ever since the far side of Emu, over six hundred miles away.

Still struggling along westwards, with every irregularity in the uneven ground that jarred the vehicle being magnified greatly by our solid mulga log springing arrangements, we noticed a dozen yards to our right a clump of spinifex beaten down flat. This was followed by another until we saw a whole row of them in line. I could hardly believe my eyes as I pointed them out to Anne and veered over to them. There, at long last, were a set of deep wheeltracks which were not our own. Even Anne was more than mildly impressed by this latest discovery as I plotted the location of this joining-up point on my map with a note of the speedo reading and the directions of both our courses.

This had occurred within ten miles of starting off for the day from our camp at the two-hundred-and-sixty-mile point from our bulldozer and I thought that we had slept probably within several hundred yards of the Perth survey party's tracks. These astrofixes certainly took the luck out of our expeditions and made the results a certainty, although as before, those results were received with much enthusiasm.

We were now on a set of tracks which we knew originated at the sandalwood road from Laverton, and this would help considerably with the negotiations we would obviously be forced to make for petrol. The gauge was already showing only half a tank left, with fifty miles left to go, not counting the extra eighty miles to reach Laverton on the sandalwood track. This was a road made by old Martin Cable who cut sandalwood from an area near a salt pan named Lake Yeo, a hundred and fifty miles N.E. of Laverton. Based at the ghost town, he brought the logs back from Lake Yeo by Rover and tow cart or truck and on to Leonora at the head of the railway line a further eighty miles by road. I gathered they were used as incense burners in the East Asian areas and had the quality of repelling moths. It was said that a length of log placed in a wardrobe would render it free from clothes-eating insects indefinitely.

As we travelled along the survey party's wheeltracks, with fewer glances now at the Rover compass, an amazing thing happened. I looked up from studying the petrol gauge later in the day to see a truck coming towards us, still half a mile distant. It was the first vehicle other than our own we'd seen for altogether six hundred miles since leaving Warburton and as it strained and groaned along, so did we, gradually closing the gap. My thoughts were fully occupied with petrol but Anne began to panic. Asking what the reason was for the terror in her eyes she burst out with, "Goodness—my hair must look a mess."

She frantically searched in one of her mysterious dilly bags and began combing and brushing at a great rate while I could not stop laughing. The expedition into the six hundred miles of unknown bush, the running out of water and petrol, the leaking differential, engine trouble and broken springs had left her quite unruffled, but here was something really big.

The two Lands Department drivers were as astounded to see us as we were to see them and asked where on earth we'd come from. On the other hand I knew where they had been and with a grateful eye to their load of petrol drums the conversation quickly got around to that. Most of the drums were special helicopter fuel but in no time we were pumping our tanks full from the rest. Actually I didn't wish to take any more than needed as I was heading for supplies myself, and they were on their way back to Neale Junction where it would be wanted.

As we both drove off on our separate ways I thought that one day's delay on our trek from the camp would have been enough to cause us to miss them. Conversely, if they had set off a day earlier the same would have applied. There would now be no need for further petrol worries.

Another fifty miles and two more days' travelling put us out on the Yeo road which was more than just a set of wheeltracks. A road patrol grader from Laverton had been over it, leaving a smooth hard surface which was very easy to accept after the last six hundred miles. Connie, alone, didn't think much of it. She immediately began to cry, no doubt thinking something was wrong because of the change from the usual bouncing about in her box.

With all this civilization about, we covered as many miles in the hour of daylight left after meeting the graded road as we normally did in a full day's bushbashing and I decided to camp before making our entrance into Laverton. Anne wondered what I was stopping for until I explained we had thirty miles to go, and being dusk, would camp in the clump of mulgas which I had seen. Here she once more looked very concerned, so I asked what was worrying her. The reply I got set me laughing again, as she said in an incredulous tone, "But we can't camp here on the farmer's land without first asking him!" She was back in England in the fields thinking about poachers, so I told her I would be only too pleased to interview the "farmer," but for one thing. The station owner, if one existed, might live anything up to a hundred miles away, and I convinced her that he would be sad if we *didn't* sleep on his "farm."

I put up the aerial to have a sked to Scotty for any exchange of news and after making contact his first transmission roused Anne from her thoughts about our lack of ethics concerning the farmer and cheered us both completely. Bonnie, the dog, had been waiting by the bulldozer that morning for someone to appear, fifty-five miles from the spot where we lost her tracks in the bush after the signal pistol shots. Two weeks had elapsed in the meantime and apparently she had been kept alive by the many pools of water from the same rains which we'd run into at the gloomy camp. She had heard the sound of the big diesel motor in the otherwise quiet bush with her sensitive hearing and made for it, but had not travelled at all on the freshly 'dozed road behind. No tracks were left and she might have picked up the first faint sounds from any direction before homing in on it, the whole operation taking two weeks. Scotty told us she had lapped up a hundredweight of food when he took her back to camp but was otherwise unhurt from her lone journey, which could easily have added up to a great deal more than the straight line distance of fifty-five miles.

Next morning Laverton came into view with its dozen or so buildings, and we drove into the main street, a dirt strip edged with a concrete kerb. In seconds the whole town knew of our arrival, and while we were at the post office collecting what mail had been re-addressed there for us, their old fashioned telephone tinkled. It was old Don Leahy who ran the two storey hotel opposite and had recognized our Rover, saying to come on over for a "feed" as soon as we were free. I'd met him four years before when passing through on my way back to Warburton after the expedition we'd made for the first time across Australia, which had been the forerunner of the Gunbarrel Highway.

Soon we were installed in the large old-fashioned kitchen alongside the big double wood stove and while the women folk took possession of Connie I clumped in my hobnailed boots still caked with dried mud over to the fire to have the usual yarn to Don. The policeman arrived to join the group, and they received first-hand an account of my new project about which they'd heard so much on the bush grapevine system. Everyone in the west had been speculating on this new road "Lennie's Gunbarrel Mob" was "pushin' through" and the versions of where it was to come out varied to the extent of hundreds of miles. Eventually someone produced a torn and dusty map of Australia, and I marked up the proposed route with a stub of pencil supplied with it, spread out on the massive bush kitchen table. When finished, this map became the most up-to-date one in existence, and it was returned to the wall with an extra supply of pins which I found in my survey bag.

Baths were offered, and a meal in the kitchen fit for any explorer was had, after which, with a promise to call again after collecting more stores from Leonora, we returned to our beaten up Rover outside and slowly drove away from the small gathering. As the policeman was present, we made an elaborate turn around the silent cop sitting almost buried in the dust at the intersection of the main street and the Leonora Road. It was the first thing Anne had pointed to with amazement as we trundled in a few hours before.

As we stood in the store in Leonora, after another night's camp, with our list of supplies to order, a man standing alongside suddenly turned and slapped me on the shoulder and called me by name. Anne accepted it as normal by asking the ceiling in general if there was anywhere we could go where we were not known, but I was at a complete loss as to who this latest friend or foe could be. He turned out to be Eric James, the manager of the organization which was again helping us, having already done so before when I had needed replacements for our trucks and machinery during the construction of the Gunbarrel Highway. Known locally as Mr Fixit, he had helped me after the first expedition across Australia, when I had passed through Leonora on my way back via Laverton to Warburton.

I told him of our latest project, quite unnecessarily, as he already knew, like everyone else, and I was assured of his further full co-operation for supplies. In no time Anne, Connie, and I were installed in his home, where his wife gave Anne all the practical help needed with Connie. Their washing machine was soon the centre of attraction and working solidly on the contents of the plastic bucket. Then came the all-important repairs to the survey Land Rover. Eric and I made our way to the garage which was well-equipped to handle everything wrong with bush vehicles. I told the owner there of the leaking differential and explained that although the mulga log springs were quite strong, perhaps regular ones could tend to even out the spinifex a little. I went on to list the wounds suffered by the Rover in our last six hundred miles of bushbashing and finished by asking him to look for any others while he operated on it. A message to Perth for all the parts required was on its way in less than an hour and as soon as they arrived he would attack the vehicle with all his mechanics. Meanwhile I could use it as it was.

It reminded me of the new car I had bought in Adelaide, assisted by my little friend, Esther, and how I had returned it several months later for another new one. The manager had wondered at the short time I'd been in possession of it, inquiring why I was buying another so soon. I explained to him that although I wasn't particularly concerned at the way the back floor became submerged under four inches of water every time it rained, I did think that not being able to drive it under ninety miles an hour was little dangerous. Understandably he looked a bit alarmed until I explained that I had slowed down to a hundred miles an hour in the city, and that it was at present doing seventy as it stood, back in the showroom. I remembered how he had glanced at the speedo needle, indeed indicating seventy, when I asked him how far he thought it was from there to Salisbury. I agreed with him I also thought it was about twelve miles, but then I pointed out that the speedo showed it to be five thousand seven hundred and eighty.

He was becoming dazed and eased himself on to a chair. I tried to cheer him up by telling him the car was made of very strong material. At this he looked relieved, but I'm afraid I spoiled it a little by saying that it must be, as the tail shaft which had been rubbing on the underside of the flooring for three months hadn't even worn through. By now he was mopping his neck with his handkerchief, so I hastened to assure him it was well designed. With an almost inaudible whisper he said the firm did think of the best ways of doing things, but as I went on to tell him happily that I liked the way the door handles always fell off on the inside and were easily found on the floor or under the water, he began to whimper. Coming to his aid, I told him that although the knobs broke off one by one from the radio, I didn't mind a bit. I could easily tune it with pliers.

By then I was doing my best to console him, as he blew his nose, but discovered I was losing ground after gently telling him how, with the screwdriver always at hand, I could replace the sunvisor without any trouble at all when it worked loose every hundred miles.

Another salesman had by now appeared and with his arm around the manager's shoulders, began to soothe him as I explained to him that I had only come in to buy another car. I just had time to point out that the water on the back floor helped rather than hindered us, as most of our long trips were done in the hot weather, and the passengers could keep cool by paddling their bare feet in the main stream. The luggage on the floor could be kept dry by placing it on top of several small boulders we had strewn about for the purpose of keeping it up out of the waves.

Even this hadn't helped, as the salesman began to look as forlorn as his boss, so after ordering a replacement car I had left in somewhat of a hurry to give them time to compose themselves before the next customer arrived.

Our Land Rover was reduced to this condition here in Leonora, understandably in view of where we had driven it, but the bush garage mechanics were hardened to tales of woe and looked upon it as a challenge to their ability.

Within three days the survey wagon had been restored as good as new, the extra twelve gallon drums arranged by Eric had been filled with petrol, and the washing dried and packed back into our old army steel ammunition box. The rations, including a gross of eggs, lay in a heap outside Eric's store among the many other bundles of supplies labelled and left for their owners, as it was now the weekend. It was refreshing to see all these goods left lying about, in the confident knowledge that none other than their owners would touch them. They came in from the bush to collect what sometimes had been ordered over the flying doctor transceivers. I wondered how long they would remain safely awaiting collection in the cities.

The petrol drums were wired on to the roof, and Anne and Mrs James gave Connie her last proper rinse for many months to come. A small amount of water in a bucket would have to do after that at about fortnightly intervals. During our stay we had learnt of the proximity of the sheep station owned by our good friends Bob and Flo Crombie, who had run a similar station near Woomera from long before I had arrived to start surveys for that project. They had since moved over to Western Australia to take up Morapoi, and this was only fifty miles away from Leonora. Having contacted them through Eric, we had been ordered to call in on them on our way back to the desert, so with a

115

farewell to Leonora and all the people who had so readily helped us, we drove slowly out from the main street.

On the way to Morapoi I told Anne we'd stay the night and continue on to Laverton in the morning, at which news she was aghast. We couldn't possibly move in on people like that unless formally invited weeks before! I could see we were back in England once again, but when we pulled up outside the homestead, our wild reception by Bob and Flo at least added to her Australian outback education. I hadn't seen them since they'd moved, and it was really a welcome to dispel any of her fears about our sorry lack of "correct procedure." It wouldn't take long at this rate to turn her into an Australian. Connie was commandeered, wide-eyed, by Flo, who repeated that she also never thought she'd see the day, and at once we were shown where we would be sleeping.

Until late into the evening all our news poured out, on both sides, covering the previous fifteen years, including the time we had dug out the tightly packed saltbush from Bob's motor bike engine in South Australia to find a lost screw. I was able to tell him I still had the stockwhip he'd obtained for me from his relation, Max Scobie, (on the Birdsville Track) who had made it, and on and on it went, while Anne was informed in detail about my bushranging past by Flo. Barry, their son, who was four when I first saw him, was now a grown youth and just as likeable as he had been then. In the morning Anne had to add her name in pencil to be later stitched on to Flo's table cloth, containing thousands of signatures of everyone who had enjoyed the Crombies' hospitality during the early Woomera days. It had been signed by Royalty, Governor-Generals, knights, lords, test pilots, scientists, and there was even my own insignificant signature which had been one of the first on the almost blank square of material, over fifteen years before.

Soon after, we were again sadly on our way, and camped at dusk near the ghost gold mining town of Morgans on the Laverton road. Anne had fallen asleep even before I finished telling her about the fist fights which used to last there for three weeks at a time when Morgans was booming.

The head of the road, and the start of another long, lone survey ahead

My "oasis" at the bald rock mountain wasn't as mythical as the camp had imagined

BACK TO THE BUSH

ALTHOUGH MORGANS SHOWED ALL THE SIGNS of having been a roaring gold settlement in its day, it was now just a ghost town. Here and there stood a wall. One still had the word "Bank" on it—just discernible on the faded paint work on the crumbling masonry. Another building, labelled the Municipal Chambers, had no windows, but it had obviously once been an attractive piece of architecture.

The mine manager's house had been built on a hill overlooking the goldmines, and from its once fly-wire protected verandah there was an unending view of mulga scrub as far as the eastern horizon. The western aspect was blocked out by a rocky face in which a cave had been made to serve as a cool room. A large packing case in the shape of an upright piano stood on the back verandah. Although it was eaten to shreds by white ants, we could visualize the times when sing-songs and dances around its contents must have been one of the main entertainments.

The shell of an old black Model-T Ford lay among the saltbush nearer the main shafts sunk into the Pre-Cambrian rocks which still existed under the wooden derricks and rusty machinery. The chemistry section must have been the

The "stolen" town we used as the rail siding for the Maralinga
   atomic project

The grader, too, became bogged at the bald rock mountain

area with the dozens of graphite crucibles among the ruins. It seemed amazing that all this should have been left to the mercy of the elements when the gold had run out.

Back at Laverton once more Don had us in the kitchen for the midday meal. There we met another old friend of mine—Graham Canning—known locally as "Snow" because of the colour of his hair. He had been with the rescue party that had come out to me from Maralinga at the time when I met that miserable-faced dingo. I hadn't seen him since then so we had plenty to talk about.

After dinner we called over to the local store to refuel and make last-minute preparations for our return to the camp. Executing another turn around the dust-covered, concrete silent cop, we drew alongside the hand-operated petrol bowser, and a boy ambled out of the store to help us. I climbed up on to the roof of the Rover above the level of the pump and began to untie the ropes holding the drums Eric had given us at Leonora. I could then put them on the ground to top them up with petrol. The boy asked what I was doing. When I explained, he told me that I need not get them down as the pump hose would easily reach up into them. However, I pointed out to him that although the hose would reach, the petrol would not flow into them up on the roof, but he told me that of course it wouldn't as he had not yet pumped any into the glass bowls on the bowser. I explained that even if he had, the fuel still wouldn't run up the pipe and into the drums. He looked at me with pity and assured me it would as it always had before, but I still tried to convince him that liquid just doesn't flow uphill. He begged me to try it and see for myself, so feeling as silly as I must have looked, I placed the nozzle in the open drum. Before pushing the lever over, he explained it all carefully in one word: "Force." He accompanied the word with an upward thrust of the palm of his open hand as he triumphantly released the lever to the open position. Nothing came out, and I stood holding the dry hose, hoping that no one who knew us was watching.

At this he became bewildered and began scratching his head, his fingers disappearing into his shock of curly black

118

hair, meanwhile telling me that "force" had always done it before. Giving up the problem, he reached up for the hose and said perhaps it might be better to untie the drums after all. Before handing the nozzle down to him I tried to convince him that the petrol would come pouring out unless he moved the lever to the shut position, but once more he assured me it wouldn't, and pointed to the dry end I was holding. As nothing would convince him that he was on a level lower than the glass bowls, I handed the nozzle down, whereupon the petrol came gushing out and ran along in the dust, the boy holding the nozzle up like a vertical fountain. Petrol was cascading over his arms as he tried to stem the flow with his other hand over the end, but it was welling up through his fingers, until I mentioned to him him that the flow might stop if he were to close the lever. For once he agreed; he thought it was a wonderful idea, and admonished himself for not having thought of it.

By then I had the drum loose. I climbed down, carrying it on to the level to start the operation over again, and we pumped the bowl full. Soon it was topped to the brim, and then some went over the top before the boy got around to working the lever again. By now we were all sloshing about in the petrol-soaked mud around the pump with the ants floating along in the main stream. At least the drum was replenished. While I hoisted it to the Rover's roof I asked the boy if he would also fill the main tanks, so I opened the caps for him before climbing back up to re-tie the ropes. As they only needed topping up—a fact I apparently hadn't made clear to him—in no time the petrol again came surging out around the hose from the full tank as the boy tugged the nozzle out of the opening to hold it up, once more allowing the fuel to spurt out all over him and back on to the dust. I wondered how the store ever made a profit on its petrol sales. I called to him to shut off the lever, and as though it had just happened for the first time he slowly reached for it saying: "I never thought of that."

With the tanks and drums eventually brimming over, I drove the Rover a few yards away out of the fumes and petrol mud before Connie passed out. Then there was the job of working out how many gallons we'd taken. The boy worked it out quickly at ninety-seven gallons, but I explained that that was more than all the containers put together held, even if they'd been empty to begin with. After another quick calculation, he said we'd got fourteen gallons. Anne thought that was quite a difference, so I said it was more than that as the drum alone took twelve. He thought again, and arrived at the figure 'fifty. I looked at him silently and slowly shook my head. So he asked me what we had got. I told him thirty-three, including the supply in the dust on the ground, so we all went in to fix up the paper work. As we drove slowly along to meet Snow, who had asked us to stay the night, we heard the boy saying to the bowser as he stood staring at it: "Force always worked before."

The next morning before pulling out, we returned to Don Leahy's place where an old bushman sat on the verandah in the sun on his favourite box covered with sugar and flour bags. He asked me if I was one of "them guviment grologists" looking for Lasseter's gold reef. Recently, someone had passed through Laverton, complete with four pegs and a length of wire to mark out his claim . . . when he found it. I hadn't met the old bushman before, so I told him who we were. I don't think he heard me for my words were lost in a spasm of his coughing. When he paused for breath, he told us that he was suffering with "bronnical trouble," probably caused by breathing that "hydrochronic acid" he'd been soldering his tin basin with. Studying my great hobnailed boots he went on to ask me if "them blutchers kep pinchin' " me. We might have been there listening to him for hours if Don hadn't come out to rescue us. After the usual mug of tea in the kitchen with the local policeman, we all clomped outside to make a start back to camp. Old Martin Cable was there and I congratulated him on his sandalwood road to Lake Yeo and his outstanding ability to improvise in the bush when he was in trouble. We had been told that once, when he was returning to Laverton in his Land Rover pulling a big wheeled cart of sandalwood from his camp the back axle housing on his vehicle had broken up. Unhooking the cart, he had taken the whole rear assembly off the Rover including the wheels, and replaced it all with the axle and cart wheels from the dray, attaching it to the springs with wire. He had then driven a hundred miles back to Laverton in front wheel drive with the rear of his vehicle raised to the much higher level of the old iron cart axle. This was the last time I saw him, for he was reported years later accidentally killed in the bush.

Being a practical man, he asked me on this morning how I guided the bulldozer through the scrub when making the roads, and I told him about the signal flare pistol. Within minutes the group had all gathered in the main dusty street as I unpacked the large bore hand-gun and gave a demonstration to the town in general of how it worked. After the first shot was fired a wild cheering went up as the red ball of fire reached its peak and returned to earth, heading straight into a fowl run behind the post office. Everyone raced over to put out the blaze and quieten the hens after which the policeman handed me another shell from the box and the performance was repeated. This time the flare landed on the roof of the store and I was thankful the rivers of petrol had since dried up. A pause to shovel up dirt over it from a truck, then more shots, finishing up with the policeman trying his hand. This shot roused a sleeping dog a hundred feet away, and bounced along the dirt to land in another fowl house, much to the excitement of its inhabitants and the townsfolk.

After that we restored the gun to its box, and shaking hands all around, Anne and I once more slowly went on our way. We felt we had been accepted by Laverton and its lone police force. Soon the group was lost to view in the billowing clouds of dust always present behind a vehicle on a bush road. As we headed for the quietness of the Great Victoria Desert and our camp, the last person we saw was the petrol pump boy still scratching his head.

That night, we camped among the sandalwood trees by Lake Yeo near Martin's camp on his road, at a place called Point Salvation. There we erected the aerial for a sked to the camp to inform them we were on our way back.

After leaving the sandalwood road the next morning, at a

121

distance of about ten miles a huge box-like structure appeared above the scrub ahead of us. The mirage made it appear to be unconnected to the ground. We decided to head for it on our way to the Moreton Craig Range which was not yet visible.

It took an hour of bushbashing to draw near to it, and it wasn't until we broke out of the mulga on to a gravel flat that we saw what it actually was. The gravel swept up to a high mount in one place on top of which was a rocky flat-topped hill with vertical cliffs all around. This was all that could be seen above the level of the trees. It would have been almost impossible to climb, but the square top appeared to be on a level with the top of the Moreton Craig Range which was now only a mile or so to the south; the two must be made up of a similar geological material. Only the intervening country had been eroded during the millions of years; the two rises had resisted the weathering. It was quite an exciting find. But we were anxious to keep moving, as we still had three hundred miles to go, so we made immediately for the main range and were soon on top, exploring the country to the east with binoculars.

It was growing dark once more. I manoeuvred the Rover so the square-topped butte was framed in the rear doorway of the mattress room. Soon we had a large fire going, and Anne prepared Connie Sue's tea. We were back in the unbroken country where we were to stay for the next three months during which I hoped to make at least five hundred more miles of road. The plan was to bring the road as far as Neale Junction, from there up to Warburton, and down to Rawlinna—quite an ambitious programme including the surveying and astrofixes. The remaining distance from Neale Junction to the sandalwood road leading to Laverton was the last section, and I hoped to be able to make it using only the grader, as I aimed at sending the bulldozer back east by rail as soon as we worked it right into Rawlinna. If everything worked out, that year would be one of our hardest, but most productive, as two more roads would be opened up across our country's expansive outback.

Before climbing out of the Rover next morning we could

see the most impressive spectacle of the square hill with the sun beginning to rise behind it. I'd arranged the camp for that purpose; Anne was suitably impressed, but Connie's only thoughts were for her breakfast, so we placed our billy of ice on the fire.

We were soon on our way, battling through some of the thickest scrub we'd seen. It had grown that way because of the quick run-off of the scant rains over hundreds of years flowing down the gravel rise to the base of the butte. The water had washed any seeds into the area circling the hill and subsequently supplied them with the moisture resulting from those rains; the effect was an almost impenetrable circular barrier of mulga protecting its centre structure.

As we drove south around the end of the Moreton Craig I began to keep a sharp lookout for the wheeltracks from our westward expedition to Laverton. According to my calculations, they should have been about twenty miles to the south of our present position. After driving to Laverton I had decided to make more use of Martin Cable's road by veering my road up to join it instead of paralleling it for fifty miles, a dozen or so miles to the south.

Sure enough, at a speedo reading of eighteen miles from our previous night's picturesque camp, the wheeltracks appeared. I knew that if I followed them east for nearly three hundred miles I would arrive at my camp and the bulldozer. The inspections of the Rover compass again became less and less, and we settled down to try to traverse this distance as quickly as the spinifex would allow. Connie was again in her element, rolling about in the tea chest; in fact by now the movement must have appeared quite normal to her. What was really unusual was when it was still.

Several flat tyres had resulted from the mulga barrier around the "box" hill, so we decided to mend them at a dinner camp in the warmth of the sun for a change, instead of by the firelight when it was freezing. Anne cooked some more of the gross of eggs we had brought from Leonora; Connie wasn't sure what they were as they didn't come out of the usual little tin. Another day of this dragged by until we saw a vehicle approaching on the same wheeltracks.

It would be a Rover attached to the survey parties at Neale Junction and one of the group which had been fuelled by the same truck we had fortunately met on our way out. It didn't take us by surprise this time: Anne was slower reaching for her brush and comb.

It was Chris Henderson from the Perth Lands Department who had learnt from the truck drivers all about our movements, and he drew a map in the sand where the survey camp was located. More important, he mentioned that they had boxes of air photos of some of the areas in which we were working and I was pleased at last to be able to make use of these, even if they only covered a small percentage of my programme.

On the following day, we first made contact with their main camp, and it proved to be a great occasion for us all. A brightly coloured helicopter stood nearby in a clearing, and Anne and I cast many longing glances at that, after crawling over almost nine hundred miles of spinifex-covered sand ridges and through thick scrub to carry out a survey which could have been done in days with such a machine. Our actual work would have to be done on the ground, day by day, guiding the bulldozer, but at least we would have known of the obstacles across our path by this easier method.

At the camp we had access to the air survey photographs, and with the willing co-operation of the Perth surveyors in their camp we extracted a selection of photographs which overlapped each other and covered the country towards Warburton for the first fifty miles. This was the area we had battled through over the worst of the sandhills and we were delighted to see these photos: I could plan the course of the road through the maze each night, and providing I knew where I was on each photograph, to a needle point, all the time, the resulting road marked on them could be transferred to the new maps. Also, with this help, I could see the completion of my programme for this year becoming more of a certainty.

By now Connie had been able to restore her strength once more with a mixture of hot water and milk powder, and so with the selection of the photographs safely tied up between covers of heavy cardboard, we left—we still had to travel a hundred miles east to reach our camp. It had been a much more successful meeting than I'd imagined, although we had all known it would take place sooner or later as a result of repeated astronomical observations for latitude and longitude, as we beat our way for months slowly through the bush. It was a case of "it takes a surveyor to catch a surveyor."

WESTWARD HO! THE 'DOZER

WE ONLY MADE TEN MILES before camping that night. The
next morning we awoke to the sound of the wind rustling
in the mulga branches. It was August, and wind storms
could be expected at any time. As usual I looked for evidence
indicating from which direction it was coming and was sad
to see the loose clumps of tumbleweed bouncing along the
ground towards the east. This meant we were to have a
strong tail wind and in turn a constantly boiling radiator as
we slowly made our way along.

Sure enough, as we drove the temperature gauge climbed
to well past dead hot in minutes and the engine began to lose
power. There was nothing else for it but to turn the vehicle
around into the wind until the needle returned to normal,
and then carry on once more. The entire day was made up
of making a mile or so progress with the wind, turning into
the wind, and repeating the process according to the temperature needle; consequently we only gained twenty miles
the whole day. We would alternate the left hand circles with
right hand ones to stop Connie becoming too dizzy. The
wind died overnight. It was the forerunner of the ones to
follow; they could last anything up to a fortnight.

As we neared the eighty-mile reading, we heard the first sounds of the diesel engine on the 'dozer. We stopped and cooked more eggs. We seemed to be having quite a number of egg dishes lately as they were so versatile, and now, as we were within earshot of our camp, we began to look forward to Paul's variations. For interest we counted what was left of the gross of Leonora eggs and found to our surprise that we had eaten our way through eight dozen during the week. After all, ten-egg omelettes did taste rather good!

It wasn't long before we caught sight of the dust cloud indicating where the bulldozer was working, and soon we were asking Scotty how everything was going. It was reaching the time to stop for the day so he switched off the machine and accompanied us in the Rover back to the camp along the new road which strung out behind the great sand-polished blade. He had done well, and was still right on our tracks. We all yarned around the fire that night about events since we had parted about three weeks before.

Bonnie came racing over to our Rover before we pulled up in the camp; it was the most exciting welcome anyone could have expected since Warburton. It was impossible to do anything other than fight her off as she leapt up to us, licking and yelping until out of sheer exhaustion she subsided and we could at last climb out of the Rover and walk over to see the others. Everything was as it had been, and we were pleased to be home again after all the long and hard travelling we'd done. Soon we were once more sitting at our bush table having a meal—but not of eggs.

We all sat around the fire until late into the night, talking over the events of the last few weeks, finishing up with the announcement that we had in our possession a set of aerial survey photographs which would help us considerably. We could describe the country ahead as far as the sandalwood road, as well as the stretch from Neale Junction to Warburton, but the two hundred miles south to the Nullarbor Plain was unknown ground as yet. I would tackle that after reaching Warburton via the still undetermined location of our main and branch road intersection at the Neale Junction. The exact location of the cross-roads would depend on a long and careful study of the air photos.

The next day was warm and still, and as we planned to move the camp to the head of the road thirteen miles west to the 'dozer, Anne decided to get to know the dog again by walking along the road barefoot in the soft dust with her. It would be a welcome change from straining along over the endless spinifex in the cabin of the Land Rover. We were to pack up, drive on past her when ready, and while the 'dozer was being serviced and Paul fixed dinner, I would return to collect the pair of hikers.

Eventually the three trucks and equipment pulled out on to the new road, and we all drove past them, jokingly ignoring the exaggerated hitch-hiking antics of Anne thumbing a lift. Every three miles, I left a sheet of paper with drawings of the dog with its tongue hanging out, farther and farther each time, until at the twelve-mile point the sketch showed Bonnie lying on her back, paws in the air and her tongue trailing out on to the dust. The mileages were marked on each sketch giving Anne an idea of how far she had walked, but I didn't think she would really catch up with any of them before I returned to collect her. When all was ready, I set off back thinking she would have given it up, and would be waiting under a mulga tree. I was prepared to travel twelve of the full thirteen miles to find her. I was amazed to see her ambling along, throwing sticks for the dog to chase, only four miles from the new camp.

We all settled down to the routine of making the road, reflecting sun flashes at the 'dozer from well in advance of it. While waiting for it to reach us, I checked with Maralinga on the radio about the progress of Quinny who was again on a trip back there for further supplies of fuel, water, and rations.

It was again time to cut everyone's hair, a job which I always had to do monthly and this was done in the camp after a small bucket shower had removed the clouds of dust collected each day. More sun observations followed, and when I plotted them, I discovered we were within a mile of the same latitude I'd observed when we had set off before the rain on our expedition at the point a hundred miles away.

128

This section of the road was without one sand ridge crossing and thus gave us an idea of the regularity of their pattern. Actually we were within twelve miles from being due west of Vokes Hill corner now three hundred miles behind us, and this was accounted for by the upward trend in the road to clear the Wanna Lakes. The east-west lay of the seemingly endless sand ridges was almost perfect, they were so consistent.

Then after two weeks of intensive work, during which I had decided exactly on the location of the cross roads and had discovered a further set of Aboriginal "placed stones" lying in a pattern on a stony rise, we bulldozed the road right to Neale Junction. At the sight of the flare pistol Bonnie tried to head off again, so from then on, whenever it was used, we were forced to lock her up in the Rover.

With the lead-out from the junction bulldozed a few yards west, pointing to Laverton, and a few yards south in the direction of Rawlinna two hundred miles away, we turned the heavy machine north to begin the two-hundred mile link to Warburton. We would continue on with the future lead-outs after closing the gap to the mission along the general route of our earlier reconnaissance but at least the cross roads had been established, a feat we had been striving to accomplish since leaving the Alice Springs road six hundred miles away to the east. It was a coincidence that it came into being on 16 August, the birthday of my old friend John Richmond, a surveyor in New South Wales who had first taught me all I knew about astronomy. I was able to include this news in a radio-transmitted telegram to him on that day, observing a custom which I had followed for almost a quarter of a century.

Without loss of time, I flashed a mirror to indicate our first direction, based on the air photos, and heading for Warburton, and in a mile or two we passed near the Perth survey camp. There was another lively reunion waiting, and my little group of bush bashers was equally as anxious to help them by immediately bulldozing out a petrol-loading pit for their fuel supplies. It wasn't every day that use could be made of a 'dozer in this country so this was followed by a hole for their empty tins so they could keep the flies at bay.

Soon, however, we were all on our way again, and with the assurance that their air photos would be returned complete with the marked-in road in due course, and another look at the helicopter, we pushed on north on this section of our project. That second road west across Australia would still have to wait to be finished later on.

Planning the first fifty miles of the road to Warburton was like working out a puzzle on the air photos — how to reach the end of the coverage without crossing one sand ridge. They all appeared quite clearly on the prints taken from about twenty-five thousand feet up, and I found I could run a fine line from bottom to top over each photograph, continuing on as the runs overlapped, without crossing one ridge until I came to the end of the photos I had. This fine line, if turned into a bulldozed road on the ground, would therefore be the best course to follow. All I had to do was to be sure at all times that the finished road exactly coincided with the line on my photograph. In some places this was going to be easier said than done, but in the thickest of the sandhills the points where the ridges cut out were clearly defined, and as these points were where the road was going to be, it would be a comparatively simple matter. When I reached the point where the line ran off my last photo, I planned to carry out an astrofix and continue on as usual.

We had no sooner started and were just entering the southern edge of the wild confusion of sand ridges when Connie decided that she had been lying down in her tea chest long enough. Suddenly she stood up to hold the edge of the box. It was the first time in her life she had actually balanced on one end, so we decided to call the finished road from Warburton to Rawlinna the Connie Sue Highway.

The weather was at last beginning to warm up a little and the billy of water on the roof was no longer solid ice in the morning. Quinny was constantly making regular runs to Maralinga back along the road we had just finished — one and a half thousand miles there and back — for supplies. Radio skeds with Maralinga confirmed his safe arrival and told us when he left for our camp so we could know when to expect him back. If he didn't arrive within a week of leaving,

130

we'd give him a further week after which I was always ready to go back to where he might be broken down; it might be a distance of anything up to seven hundred miles. He mostly made it, at anytime of the day or night, and when the engine first roused the camp, say at three o'clock in the morning, a billy would be on and boiling for him by the time the laden truck pulled in an hour later. I was always pleased to hear that engine as I knew it could possibly save me a thousand miles of driving and a hold up in the programme.

One day as I was pushing through the bush to flash another mirror direction to the 'dozer I felt a difference in the steering of the Rover that wasn't caused by the spinifex or scrub. Because we had nearly travelled the distance I meant to go I climbed to the roof and gave the signal over the level of the low mulgas until I heard the big diesel rev up and begin its crashing sounds as it mowed down the trees on its mark-out towards me. Then I lay under the Rover between the front wheels to examine the cause of the trouble. To my dismay, I saw the whole offside front wheel assembly hanging loose on the end of the axle housing. The studs had finally sheared off, all except one, which was half out of its seating. This was going to take some fixing. I stood up and told Anne that we were really in trouble. She looked up from her job of sewing a pair of cooler shorts for Connie out of one of my old shirts and casually asked if that were so, returning immediately to her needlework. I repeated that it was really one of the worst things that could happen. She glanced up once more, assuring me she quite believed me, and asked if I thought the shorts would suit Connie. When I persevered with the announcement that we couldn't move the vehicle any more as the front wheel had fallen off, she asked if I could draw a picture of Mickey Mouse on the front of the rompers, so I forgot about the wheel and proceeded with the art work.

It took three hours of hard work with a hand drill to remove the burred over remains of the broken studs and luckily I noticed some bolts on another part of the Rover axle flange which would fit exactly. As there were quite a few of these

131

bolts holding the axle housing together I thought three or so wouldn't be missed so "robbed Peter to pay Paul." When we were mobile once again I mentioned to Anne that we had managed to repair the damage as I drove back to camp covered in sand which had stuck to the sweat as I grovelled about under the vehicle for most of the afternoon. She said that all along she had known I would, and asked how her handiwork looked on Connie who was by then standing up in her new attire, Mickey Mouse and all. We were then half-way with the road from Neale Junction to Warburton and well past the extent of our air photo coverage.

We had pushed the bulldozed road up to 140 miles north of Neale Junction before I began to think we should be nearing our original recce tracks, made when we first set out through the bush going south from Warburton. That had been just two months before and since then two hundred and thirty miles of new road had come into existence including the survey for another two hundred miles, so things were looking good. Being early September the finish of the programme I had made for the year now seemed within our reach.

Those early wheeltracks of ours must be close as we had been roughly paralleling them since turning north but with the aid of the air photos, I had disregarded them completely although keeping a lookout for them as we went. Knowing they led right to our goal, I wanted to know at all times which side of us they were as this was one of the reasons for arranging our expedition to start from the mission.

Then one morning I began to get the feeling we'd been in that particular area before, so I mentioned it to Anne. She assured me she'd never seen the place in her life, but I told her it was close to the rocky descent which we'd slid down with the Rover after camping on the edge of the escarpment in the freezing cold on our third night out from Warburton. Just as I was giving up trying to convince her we crossed over our own wheeltracks which we hadn't seen for hundreds of miles. The feeling had been too strong to overlook, and even Anne agreed, after the indisputable tracks had shown themselves, that the breakaway country was familiar.

The waistcoat-wearers' city car didn't get very far

Some of the original bush bashers: Eric, Len, Doug, and Paul,. with the Gunbarrel grader

The memories of that wild descent down the slope put the idea of following the tracks temporarily out of the picture as the 'dozer reached the spot where we had crossed over them. While Scotty turned to clear that section of the road we concentrated on discovering another route. Here Anne made her special contribution to the project by pointing to a slope up which the road might go to reach the upper level of the escarpment where the remains of our old camp fire would still be. We drove over to it and began climbing higher and higher with no real obstruction until the slopes closed in to drop away sharply on both sides of the Rover leaving only the width of a vehicle across the top. Just past this "bridge" the tableland with our old wheeltracks was waiting, so we crossed over, turned around, and retraced the route back to the head of the road. When the bulldozer followed us yard by yard as we drove, the blade lowered after we all proceeded over the narrow bridge, and flattened the top, thus preventing the wider tracks of the caterpillar slipping out into mid-air. It solved a small worry I'd been harbouring since our outward bound recce, and I called the spot "Anne's Razorback."

It was now nearing the time when we'd be out of diesel, so rather than have Quinny drive back to Maralinga for another load (a return trip of sixteen hundred miles), we tried to reach Warburton with what supplies we had. We had placed another load there months before in anticipation of this operation and now with over forty miles to go we had come to the end of our supplies. That was right where the 'dozer would have to remain until we refuelled it.

Eric, in the second Rover towing a trailer, followed us through the bush as we retraced our own tracks back to the mission. Two or three drums brought back in the trailer would be enough to close the gap by finishing the road, allowing the heavier trucks through to load the rest of the diesel drums for our return to Neale Junction along the new road. The trailer hampered Eric's progress, and we had to wait over each sandhill for him to appear before we went on. He had our tracks to follow and could make the crest of most dunes unaided, but a tow cable helped us over the worst.

Shearing time for the camp included myself

Surveying for the layout of the Maralinga atomic testing range

There was another wild Warburton welcome as we eventually drove in, and Connie, who hadn't seen anyone but two or three people since leaving Laverton, buried her head in Anne's shoulder for protection. After rolling three drums of diesel into the trailer and refuelling the Rovers at our own dump, we returned the mile to the mission for dinner and carried on straight after as we wanted to reach our camp again that night.

When dark closed in we had still covered only thirty miles, but with the headlights and the tracks which now were beaten in by three vehicles passing over them, we kept on towing the trailer over the worst of the sandhills, past the remains of the first fire we'd camped by on our way south. The dozen or so miles after dark took until almost midnight, when the 'dozer came in to view in the headlights. We unhooked the trailer full of diesel from Eric's Rover alongside the thirsty machine, and drove off to camp on the cleared road behind it. It had been a ninety-mile return trip through the scrub for that fuel, but I was happy to think it had saved sixteen hundred.

Even at this late hour as we drove into our camp old Paul, who had heard our engines an hour before, was up to give us all a hot drink after greeting us with his usual, "Good evening ladies and gentlemen." It was wonderful to have such a good team; it made the whole task, hard as it was, become more of a pleasure and privilege than a job.

It took four days to bulldoze the remainder of that section of the road, during which time Anne was able to wait under the shade of a canvas camp sheet knitting and looking after Connie, while I plunged into the scrub each day to guide the 'dozer.

Connie by this time was crawling about between the clumps of thorny spinifex; soon she found it was unwise to touch them. The days of leaving her quietly in the tea chest had gone for good, but Paul played unceasingly with her as our meals were being cooked. The heat was beginning to make itself felt so a tent fly was needed to eat under to keep the sun off each day in the camp.

The last morning I announced to Anne that by nightfall

we would have the road completed right through, so she accompanied me to be there at the finish. That afternoon we positioned the Rover on the lead-out road from the mission, fired the last flare needed, and flashed the mirror at the cloud of dust in the distance. In an hour, the road was through from Neale Junction to Warburton, a distance of just over two hundred miles.

THE CONNIE SUE HIGHWAY

WITH THIS NEW ACCESS OPENED UP, another source was now available for supplies which could come from Giles as well as Maralinga, so without further delay, Quinny was on his way. I had radioed Giles news of the completion of the road and asked them to expect our truck for a much-needed load of diesel and petrol. I informed the Woomera base to send the usual set of teletypes to H.Q. about the finish of the new road, and after replenishing all our water tanks, we turned around to begin the long trek south. It was 400 miles to Rawlinna, half of which was over our freshly-made road, leaving two hundred miles to be surveyed and laid.

At one spot on the way down we drove west off the road at an interesting looking formation of escarpment country, judging by the air photographs, and discovered a small but rugged ravine in the cliff edge. With Connie riding on my shoulders, Anne and I climbed down to see if there were water present, but although there was none, we were delighted to find some Aboriginal ochre finger-paintings on the walls of several small caves. We would have been the first whites ever to have set eyes on them, and the thought that natives had been here in ages past made the area something to be remembered. Also possibly no one would have seen them since, in such a remote miniature canyon, and this would have preserved them from destruction.

One day, as we were waiting by the fire we had made for a dinner camp in advance of Paul's truck, we saw an extra large cloud of dust approaching from the direction in which he was coming. With the knowledge that it couldn't be the bulldozer, as that was crawling along behind at three miles per hour, we began wondering what could be stirring up so much dust, when Paul's truck came into view. The dust cloud was coming from behind it but nothing could be seen through the volumes of fine dust billowing up in a much more spectacular way than usual. As he drew nearer we heard loud banging and clattering noises above those made by his truck, and soon, as he slowed to a stop by our fire, we saw the cause of it all. He had been towing the trailer since our last sighting four miles back, upside down. With its wheels in the air, the loading was almost a wreck, although only some of the ropes holding it in place were worn through. We saw there were no folding legs left on the table on the top of the load as we pulled it over, back on its wheels with the Rover. The stove, which couldn't fall out of the back, had been taking a good share of the battering.

I went back along the road to the point where we'd last seen it on its wheels, before an ant bed had flipped it over as he drove, past all the debris scattered about. By the time I rejoined the trailer I had the Rover covered with old table legs, bits of stove hot plates, and a bent and battered flue pipe. Rex had already begun the repair operation with his oxy-welding torch alight, and soon one set of legs were in shape to replace on the table. The other end could be propped up on the second table for the rest of the year as the woodwork was quite beyond salvaging. A crowbar straightened the flue, and with a bronze welding rod the hot plates were brazed together. At first it had looked hopeless but already we were seeing our way clear. No damage had been done to the trailer. In fact, Paul remarked that he had saved wear on the tyres for a full four miles.

Soon the bulldozer lumbered in and Scotty, covered in dust, could have dinner while Rex serviced the 'dozer.

A week after leaving Warburton country, we had all struggled into Neale Junction, which now consisted of a road to the east joining on to the main Alice Springs Highway, a road north right into Warburton and on to Giles, a few yards of road south and the same west. Before starting the road south, we decided to make a little further use of the 'dozer while we had it to lead out west past some heavier scrub. After a day at the cross roads servicing the equipment, we left the camp where it was and bulldozed west towards Laverton until the machine emerged through the thickest of the bush to a relatively more open area, fourteen miles away. Then reluctantly we turned the bulldozer around after clearing the lead out in preparation for the grader to carry on when we returned with it from Rawlinna. That Laverton road would still have to wait for its completion, but having carried out the survey recce for it I knew I could carry it right through with the grader only.

The year was slipping away almost unnoticed. The harder we worked the quicker the time seemed to go, and we still had three hundred miles of road to make.

Within a day or so of the beginning of October we were back at Neale Junction with the bulldozer blade heading at last for Rawlinna siding. The heat was well upon us now, and each day Connie was having a hard time remaining white, as each day the dry dust turned her little body to a coffee colour and her face, beaded with moisture, was crimson. She was certainly having a rugged introduction to life, but was otherwise healthy and as happy as any eight-month-old baby could be. She was now living in the "Mickey Mouse" shorts Anne had made out of my old shirt.

We had no sooner started on the Rawlinna section of the Connie Sue Highway when the time had arrived once again for shearing, and as I cut everyone's hair I thought how short a time it seemed since the last session. It seemed more like a few days than a month.

Then, not twenty miles on our way, the steel cable on the bulldozer blade lift snapped and the winch brake fell to

138

pieces. Rex was along in no time after I'd returned for him in the camp, and with everyone levering and hammering we helped him restore it. The following day was accompanied by a raging dust storm and we were glad the work on the winch had come when it did, as a day later we couldn't have seen it for the swirling dirt, let alone work on it.

Quinny was on another supplies trip to Maralinga as we approached the hundred mile mark south of Neale Junction, and I learnt from a radio contact that he had arrived safely, loaded up, and was on his way back to us. Although it was a seven-hundred-mile trip via the Serpentines, Vokes Hill, and Emu as against five hundred miles to Giles, I used Maralinga, as their own stores came to within twenty miles by rail. On the other hand, fuel which reached Giles had to be carted from their nearest rail siding which was five hundred miles away.

Several days after his leaving Maralinga we heard Quinny's engine groaning along under the full load of drums of diesel and petrol, three hundred gallons of water, and boxes of rations, and as always, I was thankful that he had made it once again. As the noise grew louder we walked out on to the road to see him coming, outlined against a background of volumes of dust, but something looked different about the front of the truck. For a long time we couldn't quite see what it was. Half the front seemed to be missing, and as he drove closer we were astounded to discover the truck had no radiator at all. Where it had been was now only a gaping hole with the engine itself in full view. We were still wondering how it could go at all as it shuddered to a stop at the camp. Quinny climbed out of the cabin covered in sweat and grease and gave us a cheerful greeting of, "Good day! What are you all gawkin' at?"

He explained that after leaving Maralinga he had done a hundred miles when two of the fan blades had snapped off and chopped his radiator to pieces. Most drivers to whom this happened would have sat down to wait for help, but not Quinny. He crawled the truck into Emu by constantly pouring buckets of water into the gashed radiator, while stemming the main flow out of the holes with a

139

thick mixture of flour and water. It was only a couple of dozen miles, so he persevered until he arrived at the old atomic ghost camp. There he had visited the rubbish dump and discovered several lengths of flexible tubing we once used on the bore water distilling plant. These gave him his solution to the problem. Taking the radiator off altogether and throwing it up on the back, he jammed one hose down over the outlet on top of the engine block and trailed it around the mudguard to dangle it into the three hundred gallon camp water supply tank. Then forcing another over the water tank tap, he trailed it also around the mudguard to push it over the lower inlet casting of the engine. The leaks were all taken care of with rags and leather held tight with many wire twitches and after turning on the tap, he drove the remaining five hundred miles to us with the camp water supply flowing through the cooling jacket around the engine.

It was one of the most ingenious bush improvised jobs imaginable which had got him right back to camp with the much needed diesel to carry on with the road making. With my little camp of "gunbarrel bush bashers" made up of men like these, I always felt proud and pleased to be associated with them. I'm sure none of us would have changed places with anyone throughout, and each one of us had a high regard for the other's ability, even though it was outwardly taken for granted. They must have even had confidence in my "star gazin' " as no one ever questioned where we were or where we were going, knowing that all in good time, even though it might take a year or so, we would eventually break out of the scrub through to our destination. It took this kind of teamwork to make it possible, and the completion of each project brought us each so much satisfaction that it was enough to compensate for the rough lives we led and urged us on to even greater efforts.

That was to be the last supply trip back along the road because those two dozen drums would carry us as far as the Nullarbor Plain, where we could drive forward on a compass bearing to the Rawlinna rail siding for more. That would be our base for the rest of the year's work until we turned for home after joining Neale Junction to Laverton.

After the beating the supply truck had suffered with those long hauls, capped by the radiator episode, I arranged by radio for a replacement truck to be made available at Maralinga when we had a chance to go there and collect it. In the meantime Rex could keep the old girl going until we reached the railway by blocking off all the leaks with pounds of solder. The weather was going through one of the worst phases of the year now, with constant violent dust storms lasting for days between periods of intense heat, and even one hail storm with a deluge of rain hit the camp, turning the country into one big bog. One night the wind came during the early hours when we were all asleep. It turned our old canvas tent fly into a collection of frayed strips adorning the mulga trees after wiping everything off the table and sending the loose dishes and pans away into the bush. The only way to find them again was to drive up to half a mile in the direction the gale was headed, and collect them from where they had been deposited.

It was time once again for a last long recce survey trip out on to the Nullarbor to see if there were any obstructions for a straight line run in, so Anne, Connie, and I set off from the camp eighty-five miles north of our goal. Connie was still eating her tinned food but drinking a great deal more water than in the winter. She had survived all the seasons from ice to heat so she would be all right now until we finished off this section of the job. The boggy country hadn't hardened properly as yet but the heat and wind were quickly restoring it to its usual dust, and the flies were now constantly with us in their millions.

Not long after we had started on this expedition we broke out of the heavier scrub on to the patches of marine limestone which was the usual forerunner of the Plain, and we could observe horizons in some directions as far as the eye could see. Then, only half a day out, we saw a wall of dust approaching, whipped up by what looked as if it was going to be the most violent of the gales we had encountered so far. Everything was still and calm at the Rover, with the sun shining, but the amount of blue sky was diminishing every second, until the dirt wall hit us. We had covered Connie over with a towel and shut all the windows and vents on the vehicle tightly in anticipation of the advancing turmoil before it struck, and from that moment onwards for three hours we just huddled down and waited. The Rover was rocked from side to side on its springs as the gravel-impregnated dust lashed it with all its fury until I thought it might overturn. Nothing could be seen out of any window, and we were forced to block off the top of Connie's tea chest completely with a camp sheet so that she would not be suffocated in the powdery dust still entering the cabin. The dog pushed its head under Anne's feet on the floor and I was wondering how the camp was weathering the storm. No doubt the boys would have tied down everything movable but we'd all been through these, year after year, so it was nothing really new.

Eventually it blew itself out and we let Connie see the light of day again. She didn't think anything unusual had happened as she was fast asleep in her box thinking night had arrived, but Bonnie wouldn't stir from the floor. Anne had seen another side of what the outback had to offer but only remarked that by the time she had finished what she was knitting it wouldn't be fit to wear. Later in the day we were right out on the open Nullarbor Plain, struggling along over the stony ground, when down we sank into a bog hole caused by the recent deluge of rain. A pool of water gathered around the vehicle in the wheeltracks as I jacked it up and wedged in rocks from the plain, shovelling, and generally covering myself with mud. Even Anne got out to act as stone collector and tool washer as the shovel and jack became shapeless lumps of mud. In the middle of this Connie woke up due to the unusual stillness of her bedroom, and we decided, from her tone, that she'd like something to eat, bog or no bog.

It wasn't till the following day that we dragged ourselves into the Rawlinna siding, still caked in drying mud, and arranged for diesel and petrol to be collected whenever anyone came in for it, leaving the paper work till later.

142

They'd all heard of this road coming down from Warburton so we received the fullest co-operation of everyone. Anne thought she'd take Connie over for the nursing sister to see and was told that if she'd survived all that for almost five months, then she must be healthy. We told the Sister we gave Connie a rinse in a bucket of water every month, after which the water was poured into the radiator on the bulldozer.

We had a long way to travel back to camp, so leaving other details till later, we turned and headed north as soon as possible. Our old grader, which we had railed to Rawlinna, was there waiting for us, tied to the flat top carriage on the siding, and we planned to drive it off, replacing it immediately with the bulldozer, if we ever made it.

Two days of bushbashing passed after we again entered the scrub belt before we pulled into our camp as tired and hungry as it must have been possible to become, but at least the way was now clear to carry on. There had been nothing to prevent us from calculating a bearing straight for Rawlinna, and remaining with it for at least eighty miles, so after another of Paul's welcome teas, and bone weary as we were, Anne volunteered to book a complete astrofix that same night as I observed the stars for a latitude and longitude. From this I could compute a bearing from where we were at the head of the road which was now a hundred and thirty miles south of Neale Junction, and lay out a line of markers which would set us off on our last direction. Once started we could carry this on indefinitely, if need be in the same straight line.

As it happened we ran that bulldozed road dead straight for eighty miles, after which I came in for a certain amount of criticism from later users. They told me that all they saw out of their windscreens for days was the road in front disappearing into a hazy skyline and asked why I didn't put even one bend in it as something to look forward to. I explained it simply by pointing out that I didn't want to make Australia look untidy.

Several days later another violent storm hit our little group with not so much rain but lightning and crashing

143

thunder. Bonnie was considerably upset, thinking it was more of those signal flare shots. This country was not going to let us off till the bitter end, and the farther south we progressed with the road, the more we were open to such weather which constantly batters the Nullarbor at that time of the year.

Connie had taken to crawling right out of her box by now, and some mornings she was to be found forging her way through the array of clutch and break pedals, accelerator and gear lever, having dropped over the edge of the box to the seat and on to the floor. One dinner camp brought Scotty over to us in a great state to inform us Connie was right out of the Rover on her own, fighting her way along through the spinifex. She had climbed out of the box, edged along the mattress to drop on to the open tail board. It had then been a simple matter for her to fall the rest of the way on to the sand and head off into the prairie. It was lucky the tail board didn't happen to be over a clump of thorny spinifex as we would have been picking spikes out of her for months.

Then one day the 'dozer became bogged deeper than the caterpillar tracks in a ditch on the Nullarbor which had become bottomless mud again from the recent rains. We camped by it for nearly a week, feeding rocks collected from the plain in under the plates as they slowly turned, sucking them under. It had taken half-a-day to shovel the gluey mud away enough to first remove the blade holding-bolts, thus allowing the tractor to move more freely without the extra burden on the front. Connie added her share of stones when she saw what was needed, throwing her pebbles in with the others. Eventually, after six days of solid work, the heavy machine began to move and soon was up on the harder surface, dragging the five-ton-blade towards it by its own winch cable.

The radio aerial masts of Rawlinna were now visible across the open plain and as the blade of the bulldozer was no longer making any impression on the iron-hard sheets of marine limestone, it was raised for the last time and driven straight for the loading ramp at the siding. Rex had already fuelled and serviced the grader still waiting on the flat top and we started it, drove it off and down the ramp. Then our faithful old 'dozer trundled up to take its place on the rail carriage.

For the first time in history, a vehicle could now travel by road from Rawlinna via Warburton and Giles to Alice Springs, using a thousand-mile road made by the Gunbarrel Bush Bashers.

IF YOU ASK A SILLY QUESTION . . .

THE PLAN NOW WAS TO GRADE the two hundred miles of
bulldozed cut back to Neale Junction before turning west
from there to complete the final stage in our project with the
road to Laverton. If that were possible during what was left
of the year then we would grade right back to Warburton
mission over the road we had just made.

That left two or three weeks in the immediate future while
the grading was in progress before I would need to be on
hand to guide the grader over the Laverton section, so there
was time to collect the replacement truck waiting for us at
Maralinga. Quinny would drive his crippled truck while I
accompanied him in my Rover to ensure his ultimate arrival,
and although it was roughly the same distance, we planned to
go via the Eyre Highway. This was the only other access
across Australia except the Trans Australia Railway down in
these parts, and was a hundred miles south of the line. We
had made the first road across the centre five hundred miles
to the north, before which the only other way over was a
thousand miles from here due north through Halls Creek.

The Eyre Highway was of course devoid of sandhills,
being on the Nullarbor, and instead of returning to Mara-

linga via Neale Junction, the Serpentines, and Emu on our own road, we were pleased to use someone else's for a change. So we loaded Rex's truck with diesel drums to see us out for the rest of the year and petrol to last till we again visited the pumps operated "by force" at Laverton, and Paul's ration truck was replenished from the store at Rawlinna. Quinny and I loaded on just enough to carry us through to Maralinga.

The weather was now decidedly dead hot, being over a century each day, and we thought Connie might possibly be starting to feel a little warm. Anne didn't mind the fact that the Rover cabin thermometer showed over a hundred and twenty degrees most of the time due to the red hot duralium bodywork plus the sizzling engine adding its share, but it was Connie's vermilion coloured cheeks she was mainly thinking about. Flies were black in clouds thick enough to cast a shadow, and as I knew the following month wasn't going to improve the conditions, we began thinking of having the mini bush bashers reluctantly finish up their trip.

While we were still together, Rex thought it would be a good idea to eliminate the clattering noise which had been coming from the little refrigerator engine on the trailer before loading it with fresh rations. He said that while trying to eat his meals with it going in the camp he hadn't been able to taste anything for the noise. Although that sounded hard to believe, we all understood, somehow, although none of us ate with our ears. So the engine was dismantled enough to show that the bearings were worn out. I then realized why he wanted to do that job before we parted, and I cut the tongues out of my hobnailed boots and passed them to him to use as leather bearings . . . without even being asked.

As the grader began its work back along the new road, Quinny's truck and my Rover started south towards the Eyre Highway, and by midnight we were over three hundred miles on our way. The patched up radiator was holding, although buckets of water had to be constantly poured in, and I was thinking the improvised job with the external tubes had done a better job.

The camp that night was to be Anne's last for this trip, as

147

it was for Connie and the dog. They had been camping for five months in some of the hardest and most remote country in Australia, surviving ice cold nights through all seasons to the present incredibly hot days and had put up with dust storms, rain and mud, flies, and a variety of out-of-the-ordinary food. They would never eat herring on shortbread biscuits again, and in fact now even the sound of the combination makes Anne feel off colour. Connie had gained two teeth and learned to move about unaided, and Bonnie had confirmed her original doubts about getting involved with such a family, but everyone was as healthy as could be and still alive despite the discomforts. It had been an expedition of a lifetime, covering 8,000 miles through an unexplored wilderness of scrub and sandhills, with the nearest water often 600 miles away. They had seen over 500 miles of new road put down for the first time through those parts of the Great Victoria Desert and had experienced an introduction to outback Australia such as few Australians, let alone English people, could have throughout their lives.

We were up early in the morning, and before the heat and flies descended on us in full fury we were on our way easterly along the highway, Anne and Connie bound for Salisbury, and Quinny and I for Maralinga. After all we still had a hundred miles of road to make which would take an extra month, and after seeing that Anne and the now ten-month-old Connie were safely back, we took possession of the new truck at Maralinga. For a while we could say Connie Sue had lived half her life in the desert.

As soon as the water tank and fittings had been transferred to the replacement truck, and my Rover had been given the benefit of a full service in the well-equipped workshop at the atomic town, we pulled out on our way back to camp. It was now the beginning of November, and as we drove across the searing heat of the Nullarbor I thought that perhaps it was a good thing after all that Anne was a little closer to a water supply than camping out here in these temperatures.

I drove in front, stopping every few miles to ensure Quinny's cloud of dust was still coming, and in a hundred miles we were back on the Eyre Highway, once again heading west. The truck had a load of diesel and petrol drums, a wooden crate containing thirty dozen eggs, and a glass jar of battery acid needed to fill the several new batteries we brought for the grader and Paul and Rex's vehicles. There were cases of onions and new tyres, and altogether we had a full load of most things to last for the following month.

Then something happened which threatened our whole plan of operations. The cloud of dust was always in sight back along the flat dirt highway until one time when I searched the skyline for it, nothing was to be seen but the road vanishing into the distance to be lost in the jelly-like heat shimmer. I pulled into the side of the road to wait, thinking he might be refuelling as we had come two hundred and sixty miles and were now twenty miles west of Eucla, close to the Western Australian border. I thought of the Serpentine Lakes crossing over this same border, two hundred and fifty miles north along it from where I waited, and how I had marked it from the stars.

The time passed and still no cloud of dust until, at last, when I looked around I saw it. I was thankful I didn't have to go back to see what had happened. Just as I was about to drive off, I noticed a different coloured vehicle outlined by the brown cloud and realized it wasn't ours but someone else on their way towards Perth. As it came closer I saw it was a yellow utility van. It slackened speed as it approached and stopped alongside my Rover. The first thing the driver called out was that my mate was back along the road a bit. I thanked him and said that I supposed he was coming along soon, to which he replied with a simple but emphatic "No." Probing further, I asked if he were refuelling, and was told he wasn't and that it wouldn't do him any good even if he were, as the petrol would come out of the tank as fast as he put it in. I then inquired if he had lost a drain plug and the helpful driver again told me "No," and at last in a burst of eloquence I didn't expect from my tight-lipped friend he went on to elaborate voluntarily on the situation back along the road. "Actually," he explained, "the whole truck is upside down as I can tell easily by the tyres."

After the initial surprise at the news I asked how Quinny was and the man told me in his opinion he was still alive as he was lying on the road and he had definitely heard a groan. With that he drove off on his journey west and I lost no time in turning around and getting back to the scene as fast as the Rover would carry me. There, sure enough, a few miles back was the heavy three tonner completely upside down across the road and I ran around in search of Quinny, who was by now in a sitting position holding his shoulder. I asked him how he was and what had happened, and he explained his truck was upside down. I thought this was a good example of what you can expect if you ask a silly question but he went on to tell me he was all right other than a sore shoulder. I then turned my attention to the truck which was resting on its cabin roof and crumpled up canopy.

A car towing a caravan was next to appear. They stopped to record the event on their movie camera, while the lady opened the caravan door and soon had Quinny sitting inside as she bathed his arm and generally was very helpful. He had never had such gentle treatment, and although he kept saying he was all right, and the gravel rash would mend in time, I could see he was enjoying it. When they drove off another elderly couple arrived in their car, also on their way to the Perth Commonwealth Games, but apart from their photographing the scene they kept well away as the woman nervously told her husband to keep clear in case it all exploded.

Then came a lady in a car travelling east and after stopping for her set of photographs, I asked her if she knew she had an almost flat tyre on her car. So forgetting the inverted truck for the time being, I took out my jack and changed her wheel for her as she was on her own and didn't have any of the tools. She pointed out that she wouldn't know what to do with them if she had, so they would only be extra weight.

We then attacked our own problem. Instead of ringing for the R.A.A. I pulled Quinny's own winch cable out with my Rover and proceeded to wrap it around the whole truck until it took on the appearance of a giant cotton reel. Then attaching the free end to my Rover again I drove slowly away at right angles to the truck and started it rocking. When it was well under way I drove on, pulling the cable taut until the whole truck rolled on to its side, and before it lost momentum, kept pulling with the Rover until it fell back on its wheels. Before doing this we decided to change the back tyre which had blown out, causing it all, as we reasoned that would save jacking it up later. It was really an easy way to change a wheel and we vowed to remember what to do if we ever had a flat tyre with no jack to help us.

Then it came to loading up again, so we placed a drum of petrol at the tailboard to use as a step and started the job of putting all the heavy diesel drums back up on the tray. We had taken the smashed canopy bows off with the gentle help of a sledge hammer and towed them off into the bush. In spite of Quinny's bad shoulder we managed to get all the drums back in place, and the full drum of petrol still on the ground was pumped into the tanks, eliminating the problem of loading it up without a step. The battery acid had seeped into the box of eggs and dissolved all their shells away so we reckoned we had the only thirty dozen shell-less eggs on the whole Eyre Highway, across the Nullarbor section anyway.

So after jacking the crumpled cabin roof up clear of the steering wheel we were almost ready to continue on. The windscreen, being quite frail, had broken, and the cabin was splashed with acid from the truck battery which had already eaten large holes all over Quinny's overalls, but after replacing the spilt oil and refilling the radiator, we were surprised to find the engine worked as before at several touches of the starter button. A few other vehicles came by but once the truck was back on its wheels, we didn't merit a second glance as their occupants went straight on past with a cheery wave.

This had taken most of the day, so we only travelled a short distance from the spot before it became time to camp, as with the wind coming in through the open windscreen frame, the night air made Quinny's shoulder ache more when it was cooler. He assured me he was quite fit to drive the truck after I had asked him if he'd rather exchange it for my lighter Rover.

Another day's long drive brought us right back to Rawlinna where we replaced the eggs with a fresh supply still complete with shells, and we carried on north along our new road which had now been graded.

We caught up with the camp on the following day and were pleased to see Scotty had progressed with the grading for a hundred and twenty miles, over half way back to Neale Junction, since we'd been away. Quinny came in for much ragging from Paul who had been quick to see the condition of the replacement truck. He'd been waiting patiently for months to get back at him ever since he, Paul, had burnt a tray of almonds which he'd been roasting, to cinders and Quinny had never allowed him to forget it.

Most of our first day back was used in replacing the leather-bearing fridge engine with the one we brought with us from Maralinga, while the grading continued without a stop. There was always something to do.

Then, one camp later, as we were all asleep in the early hours of the morning, I was slowly awakened by the sound of a strange engine coming from somewhere to the south. Paul was already up as usual at five o'clock and was looking past his breakfast fire in that direction when I joined him, and we wondered who could be driving along our road as it had only been down a fortnight at the most. Suddenly we noticed a speck above the trees on the spinifex rise we had just passed over which developed, of all things, into a helicopter. It wasn't long before we were all staring at the unexpected machine, wondering who it could possibly be, when it circled and came to ground slowly on an open flat near our camp.

Three men alighted, including the pilot, all wearing sun glasses and a battery of cameras hanging from their necks. They were just in time for breakfast so Paul got out another handful of eggs. During the meal we learned they were from the Hunt Oil Company straight from Dallas in Texas, U.S.A. and had secured an oil searching lease of all the country bounded by the S.A.—W.A. border, the Nullarbor plain to the south, vaguely around Warburton to the north, and to complete their rectangle, out west to Laverton. This

152

was our first indication of their venture, and in turn they were delighted at the discovery that we had just made a system of roads which would almost exactly cut their whole lease into four equal parts. Our road from the Serpentines bisected it laterally, while the Connie Sue Highway divided it equally down the middle. They had no idea they were to be so fortunate. These roads would provide access immediately for their initial oil surveys. When they got going they would improve our little roads with an army of bulldozers and graders, but it had opened up their whole area to start them off, and they were the happiest trio of Americans you could ever hope to meet.

It was a strange meeting place brought about by the fact that they had seen our road from the air near Rawlinna and flown along it at tree top level for almost two hundred miles, until they dropped in on us. Lately there never seemed to be a dull moment. After marking up all their maps with my series of astrofixes and transferring the location of our new roads from my ragged old plans to their new ones, they returned to their "chopper" and flew off north, still following the Connie Sue Highway to Warburton. I met them all later in their main offices in Canberra at Christmas and was treated like royalty.

The day after saw us all right back at Neale Junction preparing our attack on the last stage of our year's project, which was, of course, the completion of the road west to Laverton. Half the Connie Sue Highway had been graded as well as bulldozed and with over a hundred miles of new road to make, as well as the completion of the grading of the Connie Sue to Warburton, we would be kept busy to finish it that year. It was almost the middle of November and the temperatures were becoming almost too great for the engines on the vehicles and machinery to handle.

Already it was again time to cut everyone's hair, an operation which fitted well into the plan of things at Neale Junction as we prepared for these last stages. Luckily the air photos, lent by the survey party who had long since evacuated, covered a good percentage of the country west, and I had planned the course of the road on the basis of these

153

and my two previous ground expeditions with Anne. I was glad that she and Connie Sue were out of this country right then because of the roaring heat building up to what looked like a really sizzling summer. I wrote a letter to that effect, hoping to be able to post it at Laverton when we arrived, and I was sure a handful of flies must have still been among the pages as I folded the letter before putting it in the envelope.

One day, after reaching Neale Junction, Scotty and I headed west, grading what little bulldozing we'd done when last there, and in what seemed like no time we arrived at the end of the cut where that heavy blade had smoothed the lead out into the spinifex beyond. I drove on to the first spot where I could still see the grader, and flashed the mirror back to it, being rewarded by the sound of the revving of the diesel to full throttle, and we were on our way once more.

Without those steel tracks of the 'dozer I immediately found I had to be much more selective about where I was guiding the road. Whereas the flashes could be sent back from the top of the Rover roof over a sea of thick scrub before, I now had to keep the machine in sight on the ground all the time to make sure there wasn't anything on line that the grader couldn't handle. It was more like a sensitive instrument than the lumbering bulldozer, which could bash its way through anything, and this fact was brought home quickly to us when in the first few miles of new going the front tyre collapsed with a mulga stake protruding from it.

OUT THERE NOW LEADS TO HERE

IT WAS DURING ONE OF THE DELAYS caused by the numerous staked tyres suffered by the grader that I had the first indication of an alarming story which had begun at Woomera about myself. Apparently it had gained much momentum by the time it came out there to me over the transceiver when I thought it was about time to give them a call. After the aerial was in place, I plotted our present position on the ragged old map in order to ask them to reposition the coloured map tack indicating our whereabouts and progress. Then depressing the switch on the hand microphone I called the operator at Woomera and listened for his reply. None came, so I called again and released the switch to receive, only to hear the most eerie tone I'd ever heard him use, asking in a shaky whisper if that was really my call sign on the air. I was able to convince him that it was, and the quivering voice of the operator came back through the loud speaker in a most distressed manner stumbling for the right words. "We, er, that is I, ah, well the story around Woomera and Salisbury is that everyone seems to think that you had, er, er, oh dear, well they thought you had expired!"

I came back on the air to him with a burst of laughing, and

when I was able, mentioned to him in passing that I was quite alive and asked him what had happened. He was regaining his composure a little I could hear from his next transmission and told me everyone was quite sure I had died suddenly with a heart attack. Inquiries were coming in from interstate requesting details. When he heard my radio call coming over the air he was in such a state of mind that did not expect ever to hear it again, and after turning white, thought it had come back to haunt him. I could hardly answer for laughing, which eased his tension, and I wondered aloud how such a story could have started. He didn't have an idea, but he had been flooded with teletypes as to when he had last heard from me and where I was at present lying, bleaching in the sun. Of course all he could tell them was the fact that he hadn't had any radio transmission for several weeks, which, he added, wasn't really unusual for me. But as the requests for information kept coming and his phone kept ringing with the news, he became uncertain himself, until suddenly out of the ether my call had roused him.

I was really feeling quite touched at everyone's concern, and as I wondered how the rumour could have started, I suddenly thought of Anne and how she would have been informed about it also. Such news travels fast and with the many Salisbury contacts we had she couldn't possibly have not heard, so I asked the operator if he would send her a telegram. The wording was going to be a bit awkward as I had no way of knowing how much she'd heard, so finally sent a message which read: "Roses are red, violets are blue; don't believe all that is told to you." If, by some chance, she hadn't received any indication of the expiry date, she could only think that I'd been too long in the bush.

Actually I learned later that someone who fitted my description and was living where I had stayed in Woomera, had died suddenly from a heart attack, and our identities had become confused in the retelling. Anne had been told of it all but having just spent five months out in the scrub with me didn't believe a word of it and waited for just such a message from me. The story had far-reaching results, as I was to discover with disturbing frequency when I did finally return to Woomera. Once, when I was walking along outside the store in the village there, a lady came out of the door carrying a bundle of groceries, took one look at me and dropped them all, turning light grey as she did so. She was so visibly shaken that I fought back the urge to explain to her in fun that I was really quite a friendly ghost. This was to go on in varying degrees with everyone I met who hadn't been told anything except the first part of the drama, and I reached the stage where I never knew what electrifying effect I could expect wherever I went. The most moving reaction of all came from a small girl who ran over to me near the school one morning, clutched my hand and said, "I heard you were dead and I was sorry."

By the time I'd finished this radio sked, the grader tyre that had been staked, causing the current delay, had been mended. I told the boys the news, adding how unsportsman-like I felt to disappoint them by turning up again.

Mile by mile we graded west, and the vast difference between the two machines was shown to us at every turn. Bushes the 'dozer wouldn't even notice, as it waded through, became obstacles enough to stop the grader, and the resulting road no longer fitted the name that our Gunbarrel Bush Bashers had acquired. It was a graded access never-theless and a big improvement on vehicles struggling over the spinifex and sand hummocks.

Eventually the road had progressed to the vicinity of the Moreton Craig Range, last seen on the recce back from Laverton with Anne and Connie. It was now time to alter the general course from west to northerly in an attempt to cut the sandalwood road at Lake Yeo. The staked tyres on the grader were a daily event, and as each one occurred, the mending of it left us at almost the end of our endurance, due to the intense heat. Hammering, levering, and straining with the four feet diameter tyres in temperatures of a hundred and fifteen degrees, with the tools too hot to handle, and the subsequent inflating of them, was not altogether something to look forward to so frequently. When the compressor on the grader failed it would take half an hour with the little plug-pump on my Rover to make the tyre even stand up, and while waiting for this the black mist of flies made the most of us.

Daily my detailed recces ahead of the machine took place from the time it was switched off until dark, and at last I came within sight of the box-like hill alongside which we had camped three and a half months before. We had made six hundred miles of new road in the meantime since that last sighting when the weather was at the other extreme in temperature. It was hard to imagine in this present inferno of sweat, thirst, dust, and flies that earlier the water in the billy had been converted into solid ice on the Rover roof overnight.

The dense scrub around the hill made it impossible for the grader alone to penetrate, and much as I wanted to add this point of interest right alongside our road, I was forced to skirt it outside the ring of mulga jungle. One evening just before dark I emerged from the bush, spinifex, and sandhills we had been forced to re-enter, on to the tail-end of the sandalwood road at Lake Yeo, and the recce surveys for that year had come to an end.

Without waste of time in feeling elated that the finish of our road was in sight I turned and retraced my wheeltracks back to the head of the road in the dark and was able to announce to the camp that the road would be finished on the following day. As usual, they didn't believe me, and I concluded that it must have been the way I delivered the news, grinning as I told it. Nothing could convince them once they saw that look, especially after we had all been battling towards this goal for almost a thousand miles over a period of years, off and on between the various delays. It was still too hot to sleep until late into the night but eventually the camp became quiet. The constant mending of those grader tyres in the heat had taken its toll of everyone's energy. Paul was having as hard a time with the meals, trying to keep the flies at bay as he worked, and the added heat of his cooking fire didn't help, but he kept going as cheerfully as he had from the very beginning.

As I lay on the top of my swag before falling asleep, and as the beads of sweat trickled off on to the canvas, I thought

158

how everyone would be rewarded the next day as we finally broke through.

We were all up well before the flies next morning, and after telling Paul and Rex that the camp could stay right where it was instead of moving it to the end of the road as usual, Scotty and I drove off to the grader waiting behind its bladeful of spinifex. As soon as the big diesel was going I drove around it on to my tracks made the previous evening and continued along them slowly as the grader followed. Those last few miles passed almost unnoticed with the anticipation of the completion so close at hand, and in no time I had bumped over the last hummock of spinifex and waited on the made road. Looking back to the grader creeping along in front of its accompanying dust cloud I noticed one of the trucks behind again, keeping pace with it. The boys were going to be present at the finish, and that alone was enough to show me how much of a personal interest they all had in the work, not counting the way in which the whole team had put up with all the hardships this country had to offer for so long.

With less than a chain to go, I inched the Rover along the existing road as the grader followed it in an easy curve and stopped the length of the machine short of the join up. Lifting the blade clear of the spinifex it moved back away and described a large circle to line up on the road facing the opposite direction. Then the blade lowered as the heavy grader moved slowly forward and completed the curve from the edge of the sandalwood road to the spinifex barrier. The second road made by the Gunbarrel Bush Bashers across Australia was finished on 17 November, 1962.

It was almost a thousand miles long, starting at Mabel Creek on the Alice Springs Highway, passing through the atomic ghost camp at Emu, threading its way past Vokes Hill, over the Serpentine Lakes on the border, becoming part of Neale Junction, and on to Laverton. We were still almost due west of our starting point. In one way I was sorry Anne and Connie Sue weren't with me on this day, but perhaps the achievement may have lost some of its excitement for them with this forge-like heat bearing down with all its fury on our little group of four men. At least they had been right there at the finish of the Warburton to Rawlinna road, having seen its survey and construction from the beginning, and now I could tell them about this latest in a way they would understand, having been here already on the initial survey.

To round off the job and make the most of the grader's trip back to Giles we decided to drop the blade and grade all the way back to Warburton, a distance of three hundred and fifty miles. The section between Neale Junction and Warburton would then be graded for the first time over the bulldozed cut, and back to the Junction would only be a regrade. It was a long way but if we didn't do it then it might never be done and from previous experience with this sort of operation we could have it through in a fortnight.

Leaving Scotty and the camp to start the return, Quinny and I continued on to Laverton for supplies of water and rations which were needed to carry us all back as far as Giles.

At Laverton we knew that not even the bush telegraph could have spread the news of the final break-through of the new road from the east as it had only taken place the day before, so the old map was taken down from the wall at Don Leahy's place and the details filled in. The overnight stay at Laverton was taken care of by Norman Hopkins, the policeman who had handed me the signal flare cartridges which upset the fowls on our last visit. He had some spare rooms in his local jail house and he invited Quinny and me to stay with him, to which we agreed, as long as he left the barred doors open and gave us the keys. Knowing him, we could rely on his sense of humour to make it look more realistic, spreading the story he had captured single-handed two infamous bushrangers who were staying with him as the guests of Her Majesty.

Bypassing the fuel pumps at the store operated by the boy who made so much use of "force," we went on to Leonora, after a night's sleep on the "inside," for the bulk rations and supplies we needed, and once more Eric "Mr Fixit" James and his wife helped us. Mrs James was relieved to learn that Anne and Connie were back in Adelaide and out of this

160

country, with the summer temperatures as they were, but mentioned that news had come over the air of a violent wind storm which had just hit there and hoped they were all right. I hadn't heard of this, of course, so thought no more about it.

The whole town had heard by now of the completion of the road in advance of our arrival, as the wires leading out of Laverton had been running hot since we drove in, and there followed a session of adding the new road location to many local maps. After loading up with these supplies which had been available to us ever since our leaving Maralinga three weeks before and a thousand miles away, Quinny and I drove off to Laverton on the way back to our camp.

The first thing which was handed to me at the Post Office there was a telegram from Anne informing me that in a ninety-mile-an-hour wind storm which had ripped through Salisbury we had lost the complete roof from our garage. Another night spent in the cells at Norman's "guest" house and we were again resuming our return to the camp. Driving off Martin's sandalwood road on to the curve which made up the start of ours was done with much satisfaction, knowing that if followed throughout its length, that thread of cleared ground would lead us to the established road system in the east, without the need for astrofixes or compass.

We drove along it for a hundred and seventy miles before catching up with the party already forty miles north of Neale Junction, and the new supply of fresh rations was very acceptable. It was a hundred and ten degrees each day now, and had we not been out for the year in the bush, becoming as hard as hobnails in the process, we couldn't have carried on. As it was, we spared nothing in finishing the work, and eventually within a day of the end of November the grader blade was raised for the last time that year as it tapered off into the Warburton road at the northern end of the Connie Sue Highway.

Before starting on the long trip to Adelaide, which was almost two thousand miles via Giles, I decided to install a new spring assembly on the Rover in place of the one which was broken in so many places that it allowed the wheel to

161

rub on the mudguard. It was almost a hundred and twenty degrees as I lay under the vehicle to do the job, and when it was finished, I thought again that there must be an easier way to earn a living, not that any of us would have changed places with anyone else.

As we struggled into Warburton we received the usual riotous welcome, added to by the flood of inquiries as to the whereabouts of Anne and Connie Sue. Our stay on this occasion didn't amount to more time than it takes to have a few mugs of tea, and we pressed on towards Giles, driving until midnight to cover some of the distance after the blazing sun had set. My diary entry for that day included how the engine on everyone's vehicle boiled the whole time, that the temperature was a hundred and twenty degrees, how the differential on one of the trucks had smashed to pieces, making it necessary to tow it from there on, that a tow-bar had broken off one truck, requiring a long job of arc-welding on the road to restore it, and that Quinny in trying to drag a large water-tank trailer over a sandhill had turned it upside down. As we finally camped seventy miles short of Giles from sheer tiredness, I fell asleep thinking that things could only improve, but the feeling brought about by the successful completion of our work overshadowed any of these minor happenings.

Hoping I could keep going myself, I took to driving along behind the string of odd-looking vehicles comprising our party to help see that none fell by the wayside. It was rather like coming back from a war. Several washaways had occurred on sections of the Gunbarrel Highway since we had made it, and once as I drove behind Paul's ration truck I was surprised to see how it stayed on its wheels when one side broke away some loose dirt and dropped into a water-eroded gutter a yard deep. The whole vehicle was leaning at an angle which threatened to lay it on its side at a touch, and in great haste the driver's door opened and Paul was out in a flash. The trouble was easily overcome after first anchoring the truck with a tow-cable attached to my Rover, and then by digging and shovelling under the high side for two hours until it assumed a more reasonable angle. The ground temperature was the usual hundred and forty degrees throughout this operation. We weren't going to be let off lightly until the bitter end.

Eventually each of our battered vehicles straggled into Giles, some limping along, others being towed, but at least they made it, and our faithful old grader was driven to an out-of-the-way salt-bush flat alongside the settlement and switched off. It was at last in the position—with its job done—in which I had been striving to have it for many months, as our subsequent programme called for it to be working in the opposite direction from its Christmas time resting place. Then wonder of wonders, on that first night back, clouds gathered and it began to rain, but whatever happened from now on couldn't interfere with our present feeling of freedom from the grind which had been with us constantly for the whole year. It was as if a lead weight had been lifted from our shoulders, even though to me it had been a satisfying responsibility.

It was now December, and with only thirteen hundred miles to drive home, we left Giles early on the following morning to complete the last stage of our operations. All the old mulga stakes which had been driven into the tyre covers of the vehicles in the scrub began working their way right through into the tubes as we travelled faster on the harder and more compacted roads and as always, the flat tyres came one after the other. Slowly creeping from camp to camp on the soft new road, the same tyres would last for a year.

No sooner had we emerged on to the Alice Springs Highway than we came upon a huge semi-trailer hopelessly bogged in the sand as he had driven off the road to change a tyre, so out came all our tow ropes again, and we combined all our wrecks to pull him out of it back on to the hard ground. He was having real difficulties.

After another day we slowly passed through Mabel Creek station, and I paused to gaze upon a bulldozed and graded lead-off from the highway heading away to the west, knowing full well and with a pleasant sense of satisfaction, to what ultimate destination it now led.